Variety Reduction Program

Toshio Suzue and
Akira Kohdate

Productivity Press
Cambridge, Massachusetts
Norwalk, Connecticut

Variety Reduction Program

A Production Strategy for Product Diversification

Productivity Press
P.O. Box 3007
Cambridge, Massachusetts 02140
United States of America
(617) 497–5146

Library of Congress Catalog Card Number: 89–43208
ISBN:0–915299–32–1

Cover design by Joyce C. Weston
Text design, typesetting, printing and binding by Arcata Graphics - Kingsport, Tennessee
Printed in the United States of America

Library of Congress Cataloging–in–Publication Data

Suzue, Toshio.
    Variety reduction program: a production strategy for product diversification / Toshio Suzue and Akira Kohdate.
    Combined version of two original Japanese editions: VRP *buhin hangenka keikaku* © 1984, and V*rp giho ni yoru seihin costo daun suishin manyuaru* © 1988.
        ISBN: 0–914299–32–1
        1. Production engineering.
        2. Production management.
        3. Diversification in industry.
    I. Kohdate, Akira. II. Suzue, Toshio. VRP *buhin hangenka keikaku*. III. Suzue, Toshio. VRP *giho ni yoru seihin costo daun suishin manyuaru*. IV. Title.
    TS176.S87 1990   89–43208
    658.5'038––dc20   CIP

90 91 10 9 8 7 6 5 4 3 2 1

Contents

Publisher's Foreword

This is the first book available in English on Variety Reduction Program or VRP. It combines the authors' introductory book on VRP and their VRP implementation handbook and is written for those currently challenged by product diversification in their companies. There are, of course, other approaches to variety–related problems, computer–integrated manufacturing (CIM) or a flexible manufacturing system (FMS), for example. FMS, however, is at best a passive response to product diversification. In contrast, VRP cuts to the heart of the problem by dealing with the actual products and production systems that promote diversification.

Commonality of parts means reducing the *number* of parts used, for instance, in manufacturing a washing machine casing — using three different parts instead of ten. We do this in the design stage by combining several smaller parts to make one larger part, thus reducing number and variety. We then use this same part in the manufacture of as many of our gadgets as possible. What this means to the businessman is that, while giving customers a variety of choices, we are also keeping costs down by reducing the work required.

This is the age of choice. Customers expect — and demand — greater variety and more features without extra cost. Customers are the key to survival and not one of us can afford to reduce the market's perceived value of our products.

VRP reduces the commonality of parts to everybody's benefit — buyer and manufacturer. VRP, in fact, is a program that can reduce a company's profit structure by half. By simplifying the structure of products, parts, and production, VRP can reduce manufacturing costs by one–third. VRP resolves the conflict between rising costs caused by product diversification and improved production efficiency. It is a total approach that encompasses everything from product design to production systems. VRP shifts work away from outside suppliers and improves yield.

In their professional roles as design management consultants, co–authors Toshio Suzue and Akira Kohdate have successfully applied VRP to manufacturing operations in Europe and Japan of such diverse products as auto parts, construction equipment, ships, agricultural machinery, shoes, audio equipment, prefab houses, and confections. In these instances, VRP successfully reduced material costs, processes, direct labor hours, stock in process, equipment and energy, factory space, setups, defects and repairs, management costs, and design modifications.

As an improvement program, VRP can be applied alone as well as alongside just–in–time, Shingo methods, total productive maintenance (TPM), and others. Read this book and give it to your designers, managers, and employee study groups. It will open a floodgate of ideas. I am very grateful to the authors and the Japan Management Association for inviting us to publish this work in English. They very kindly agreed to combine two books on VRP to create *Variety Reduction Program: A Production Strategy for Product Diversification* in its current form. Special thanks to project editor

Cheryl Berling Rosen, translator Bruce Talbot, copyeditor Christine Carvajal, production manager Esme´ McTighe, cover designer Joyce Weston, and the staff of Arcata Graphics – Kingsport, Tennessee for producing this superb volume.

Norman Bodek
Publisher

Preface

Every business today confronts the problem of product diversification. The Variety Reduction Program (VRP) is of particular value to any enterprise operating under the following conditions:

- As one new product after another is developed, designers continually must work overtime.
- Blueprints rapidly proliferate while personnel are kept busy feeding parts plans to the computer.
- Keeping up with parts procurement becomes a never-ending battle.
- New dies are constantly required, costs accumulate, and product life gets shorter.
- The variety of tools threatens to become unmanageable.
- Production processes become complex, their flow difficult to follow.
- Greater diversity in product type creates setup and changeover difficulties.
- Dead stock accumulates in storage.
- The number of service parts continues to grow.
- Neither sales nor profits rise in proportion to the increase in product variety.

Two solutions proposed for these variety-related problems is computer–integrated manufacturing (CIM) or a flexible manufacturing system (FMS). An FMS, however, is at best a passive response to product diversification. By contrast, the Variety Reduction Program introduced in this book cuts to the heart of the problem by dealing with the actual products and production systems that give rise to diversification.

VRP is applicable to any product in any company that is experiencing product diversification. In their professional roles as design management consultants, the authors have applied VRP to many manufacturing companies with the following products: automobiles, automobile parts, industrial vehicles, construction equipment, ship machinery, engines, agricultural machinery, measuring instruments, office automation equipment, audio equipment, welding machines, industrial robots, machine tools, transformers, control equipment, elevators, medical instruments, household appliances, furniture, prefabricated houses, electric shavers, refrigerators, showcases, shoes, and confections.

Growing international interest has stimulated the introduction of VRP seminars for clients in England, France, West Germany, Italy, and the United States. Consulting services on VRP are now available in Europe.

This introductory book on VRP results from the authors' broad experiences in industries with different kinds of products. It consists of five parts:

Part I examines the phenomenon of product diversification – why it occurs and the problems it causes. It discusses the limits of standardization and value analysis and presents VRP's objectives.

Part II establishes the five concepts that delineate how VRP defines the number of parts and processes, and how it distinguishes between necessary and unnecessary variety.

Part III explains procedures for organizing and advancing a VRP project.

Part IV provides examples of actual VRP implementation in four companies.

Part V sets out the conditions required for VRP success and clarifies potential problem areas.

The authors began developing VRP in 1975 while consultants of the Japan Management Association. Since then, the efforts of Mikio Okada, Hiroyasu Fukuda, Kiyomi Nakamori, Kazumi Eguchi, and Takahide Negishi have furthered the development of its technical applications. The process continues today.

VRP would neither exist nor continue to develop without the help of the directors, managers, and engineers whose companies provided us with consulting opportunities. We wish to express our deepest gratitude to those who made this book possible.

Toshio Suzue
Akira Kohdate
September 1984

Variety Reduction Program

PART I

Introduction to Variety Reduction Program (VRP)

Today's markets demand an ever-increasing diversity of goods. Contemporary businesses strive to meet the demands for product innovation and diversity by keeping labor costs and processes at a minimum in order to conserve their strength for future product developments.

The Variety Reduction Program (VRP) developed in response to this dilemma. VRP's goal is to lower costs dramatically by reducing the number of parts and production processes required for manufacturing a product while successfully responding to market demand for greater quantity and variety of products. In brief, VRP deals with the challenge of diversification by perfecting high-productivity products and production systems.

CHAPTER 1

The Product Glut

The diversity of products is overwhelming. Company executives often cannot say with certainty exactly what products their own companies handle. While the increasing number of products is a given in today's business environment, companies must learn to discriminate between negative and positive effects of this phenomenon. The challenge is to augment the positive aspects of product proliferation while eliminating the negative.

Handling Large Numbers of Products

A basic market reality of recent years may be described as follows: *We cannot survive — much less enjoy — consistent results without continually bringing out new products.*

Today it is virtually impossible to maintain sales at a steady level by relying solely on a market secured 10 or 20 years ago. If a company wishes to increase its sales, it must offer products that cater to current market demands. It must (1) stimulate an existing market by introducing a new model or (2) capture a new market with an entirely new product. Sales growth is contingent on the sum total of these strategies. Consequently, the variety of products continues to increase.

Looking around, we are struck by the large number of available products. They may vary somewhat in performance, style, or color, but the salient point is their sheer number. Amid this abundance, the consumer compares the features each product offers and selects the one best suited to his or her taste.

At one time, the key to merchandising was to categorize consumers by sex and age. It was enough to develop products that catered to men or women, children or adults. To those simple categories we must now add demand level, lifestyle, and regional and national differences. Merchandising today is based on the acknowledgment of individual differences, not only in sex and age, but in culture, creed, and personal taste.

In terms of products, the cultural gap between countries can be considerable. In Japan, automobile steering wheels are on the right side. In Europe, they are on the left. Cars built for Japanese consumption will not sell in Europe unless altered for export. Conversely, a commodity popular among Europeans will not necessarily be popular in Japan. The Japanese are more concerned with the mood or image projected than are the Europeans, who select a product according to individual taste.

A product in today's market must also offer something unique. A company cannot dominate sales for long without developing new technologies that respond to the constant demand for greater convenience and higher performance.

Perhaps we should restate this maxim of market pressure to say that successful development of new technology depends upon a company's ability to define its intentions and its philosophy. It is no longer a viable excuse to say, "We have a definite philosophy, but expressing it in our products through technology isn't easy." When a company develops a product, it must ask, "What can we express through technology?" This change in attitude generates new products unimaginable by extrapolation from the old perspective.

As a result, consumers, businesses, and markets alike must now deal with a tremendous quantity and diversity of products. In short, our first need is to recognize that we live in the *age of abundant products*.

Principles of Product Assortment

How do products proliferate? If we examine this phenomenon in one type of product, such as clocks or bicycles, we find something akin to a law or principle at

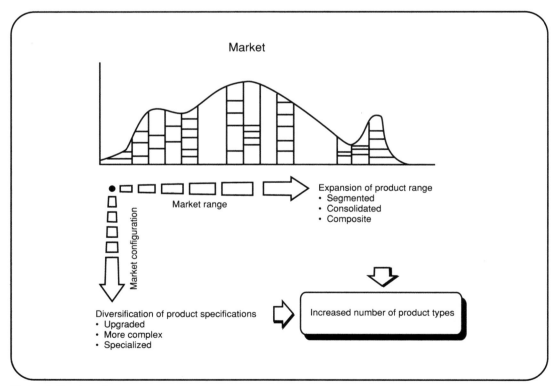

Figure 1: Product Assortment

work. This law is most easily understood if described in terms of expansion along two axes.

As Figure 1 illustrates, one axis represents a market's expanding range. Initially limited to urban youth, a product's market was gradually extended to rural areas and included all age groups. In some cases, of course, a product may acquire an entirely different market: This, too, will inevitably expand in range.

The other axis represents *segment configuration*, or the way a product occupies a given segment of a market. Here we ask how many sections subdivide a single market segment. The number of product types may vary for the same segment depending on its breakdown. By the same token, how we perceive that market will determine the features we design for a given product.

The first axis indicates the growth of a product's range, while the second axis shows increasing product specifications. In automobiles, for example, the first axis will differentiate between Toyota's Corona and Corolla, or Nissan's Bluebird and Sunny. The second axis will illustrate the different grades or specifications that exist for each car, that is, the variation represented by the DX, GL, SX, EX, or SSS.

Sometimes these two aspects are clearly defined and sometimes intricately intertwined. Together, they produce the configuration of a single product group. Achieving this configuration involves a number of different and time-consuming processes.

Let's examine the configuration for automobiles, a category second to none when it comes to product variety. First, how has the range of this product expanded?

In the past, the automobile industry followed several different policies in planning for product diversification. The first policy may be called the *upgrade principle*. For example, an automaker released an initial model in the 1000cc class. With each change in models, the manufacturer gradually increased to 1200cc, 1500cc, and so on. Eventually, the company introduced a new model in the old 1000cc class.

Now, in accordance with the *full-line principle*, the company offers a wide assortment of models to choose from, ranging from 1000cc to 3000cc, for both passenger and commercial vehicles. Figure 2 illustrates the current lineup of passenger cars. From subcompacts to luxury cars, the product range we see here is surely unrivaled anywhere in the world, a veritable consumer's paradise — assuming, of course, the consumer is a car enthusiast.

Another factor in product assortment is the *wide-variation principle*, which relates to how a given market segment is subdivided. When the manufacturer takes one car model, alters its specifications, establishes different grades, and broadens its price range, it can satisfy the needs of a consumer who may want a mid-sized car but cannot afford any options. Another law at work in today's car industry is the *wide-sales principle*, according to which the same model is distributed to several different dealers, who then sell it under different names with different external trappings.

Figure 3 illustrates this practice. Separate sales channels offer cars with different names and characteristics, but essentially identical bodies. Customers at a Vista outlet may not realize that they could have purchased the same car from a Toyopet dealer or

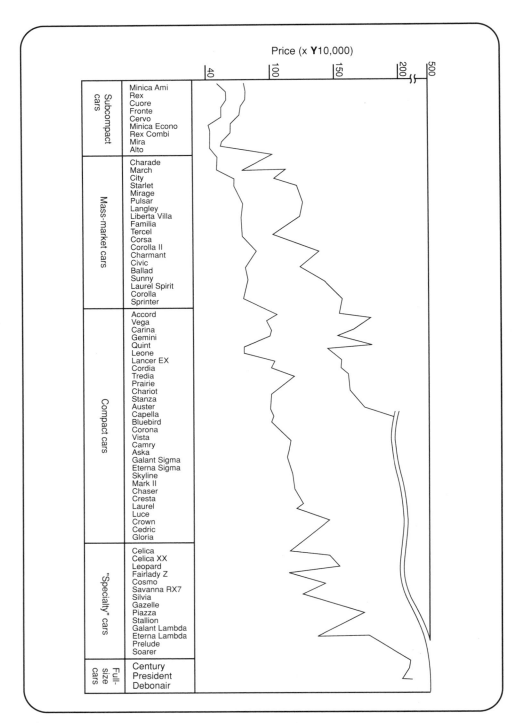

Figure 2: Product Assortment in the Passenger Car Market

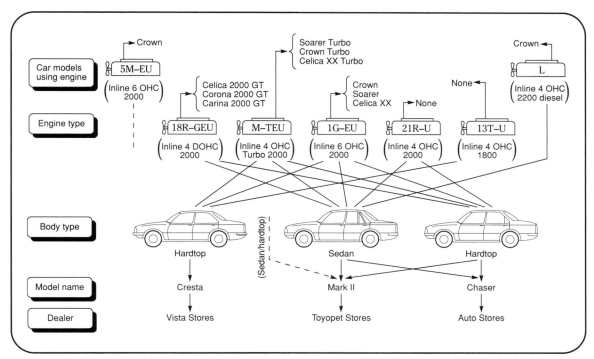

Figure 3: The Wide–Sales Principle

an Alto dealer. Or they may know this perfectly well but prefer to buy a Vista because they like the name or the style. The Vista dealer is happy because this strategy increases the chances of carrying a popular model. Our product lineup today would seem incapable of admitting a single new model to its sardine-like ranks. Figure 2 graphically illustrates this reality. Yet we know new models are bound to be introduced. Why? Because the market represented here will soon be a thing of the past. As the overall market undergoes gradual changes, so does the technology that responds to these changes. Clearly, the ways in which a market may be configured or subdivided are infinite. In other words, product variation will always increase and never decrease. Yet the forces driving product diversity lead directly to unforeseen consequences in production and business complexity.

How Businesses Become Complex

While the product lineup of the automobile market is indeed complex, certain policies at work here reveal a method to the madness. Many products, however, seem to diversify without cause. We find several different reasons for this:

1. Without a concept of "product line" or "product family" serving as a basis for development, products may be treated as separate entities. When a company han-

dles a large number of products in this individual, item-by-item manner, the result is an amorphous mass of products that by definition precludes the positioning of any one of them.

2. Products may be offered as a passive response to particular demands without an active evaluation of customer needs. Taken piecemeal, the timing of demands generated by the market is random, and a conscientious attempt to respond to such needs inevitably wreaks havoc on a company's product planning.

3. Long lapses may occur in the series development of products. If a long gap develops between the first product of a series and the second or third product, technology and market needs will have changed. The outcome is a series of unrelated products.

4. The group or manager in charge of developing each product may have differing ideas. Designers often want to promote their own ideas on product development — and this is fine if the resulting changes are integrated into the product line. Arbitrary changes to accord with a designer's opinion, however, may yield a collection of products lacking any product group consistency. In such circumstances, product assortment becomes utterly haphazard and product diversification policies turn into rationales for a jumble of diverse products.

A business becomes complex as a result of exponential growth. As the number of different products continues to snowball, so do the types of parts used to construct them. Consequently, the plant must accommodate a variety of corresponding equipment. Designers are deluged by blueprints. Purchasing departments are overwhelmed by the variety of parts they must order. In no time, an entire business can find itself buried in tasks of unforeseen complexity.

Thus, increasing product variety contains within it the elements of big problems. A policy of product diversification, however, is a necessary one. It is a means of ensuring the continuous growth of an enterprise. When such a policy ceases to be a policy and becomes instead a hit-or-miss method of increasing sales without consciously controlling expenses or giving thought to changes in the production system — a company is headed for trouble. Indeed, it will cease to be profitable. Here is how it happens:

- The moment sales growth stops, profits suddenly deteriorate and the company goes into the red.
- To increase sales and market share, the company develops and introduces new products, but sales of existing products plunge and established targets become unreachable.
- With the introduction of new products, product variety and gross sales increase, but profits drop.

- New product development and diversified production result in more piecemeal and complex production preparations, reducing overall efficiency.

What Is the Difference Between Ten Products a Month and One Hundred

The number of different product types a firm produces directly affects the production and management methods it must employ. Procedures used to produce 2 or 3 different products in quantities of 30,000 per month are not applicable to the production of 20 or 30 products in the same amounts.

If a company is manufacturing 20 or 30 products using the same methods it once used for 2 or 3, it is bound to encounter problems. Sometimes the result is meaningless capital investment. Or the company may find itself inexplicably buried in inventory. At worst, its production plants are confused by the flood of various and sundry parts needed to produce 20 products per month. Obviously, there is little hope of establishing automated, high-output production lines. Even if the company manages to set up state-of-the-art facilities for a few of its new products, the remainder are left in disarray. Ultimately, the firm cannot break even. We ignore at our peril the reality that product diversification has the secondary effect of radically altering plant structure.

The same may be said for development and design. Design methods must change from an à la carte to a full-course banquet approach. The number of products that designers handle affects the methods they employ. First, great product variety poses an organizational challenge to the efficiency of the existing structure of placing designers into separate product specialty groups. Second, in the area of production technology, every operation required to prepare for production — preparation of equipment, tools, and processes, allocation of in-plant and outside work, determination of work methods — is similarly affected. In comparing the number of plans generated for 10 products a year with the number required for 100, the difference in production work required becomes obvious.

Any enterprise that remains unaware of these realities or, even if aware, takes no steps to deal with them, is like a sick person who ignores the deterioration of his or her own health and continues to work. Sadly, there are many sick people in the workplace today.

Table 1 correlates the issues that a company or business sector confronts to the number of products and the quantity produced.

1. When both product variety and output are small, the technology inherent in the product itself sells. The issue is how to establish and refine that technology.
2. When product variety is small but output is large, improving productivity takes priority. The issue is how to supply products of consistent quality at low cost.

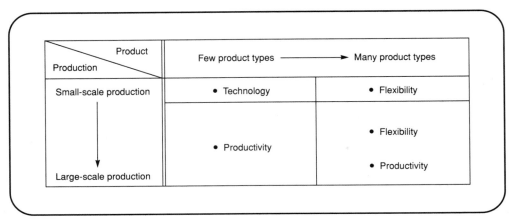

Table 1: Issues Determined by Product Types and Output

3. When product variety is large but output is small, the priority is production flexibility. The issue is how to supply the market with a large variety of products at reasonable prices when those products are needed.
4. When both product variety and output are large, productivity and flexibility take equal priority. To consider only one or the other in these circumstances is to ask for trouble. A great many businesses fall in this category.

The first step for any business, then, is to evaluate the type of workplace it finds itself in at present.

What Has Changed in the Last Five Years?

"These days, even though I pay close attention to new product specifications and make my rounds of the plant, I can't figure out our products and parts anymore," observed an executive at Company A. "Whatever we produce, costs keep going up. Our profitability has declined. I'm wondering if this might not be the time to think about how we approach our next product and our next production system. Until now, our performance has been improving steadily, but recently breaking even has become our biggest concern. I want to use this problem as an opportunity to come to grips with the development of new products and production systems."

Company A was a medium-sized enterprise that manufactured a single unit used in automobile manufacture. Sustained by the overall growth of the auto industry, it had grown steadily. But as the manufacturer of only one component, Company A was at the mercy of the whims of its clients, the automakers. Moreover, the unit design necessarily changed with the specifications for each new car model. Company A felt con-

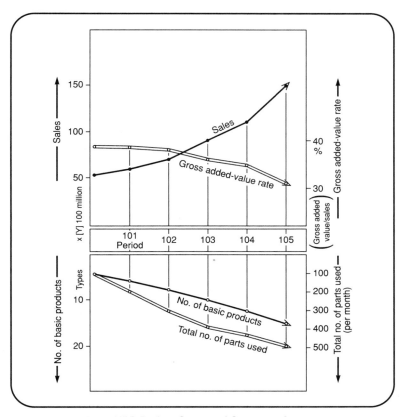

Figure 4: Results of VRP Project Survey of Company A

stantly subjected to new constraints. The problems this situation created produced the following managers' dialogue:

> *If it gets to the point where we can't break even, then there's no reason to put up with this situation.*
> *Even within these constraints, we should be able to set up a production plant that maximizes our productivity.*

At this point, the directors of Company A called consultants from the Japan Management Association to help solve their problem. After examining the state of their products and production systems, the consultants concluded that a basic reassessment of the company's design and production methods was imperative. The consultants requested that they organize a VRP project team. Company A's project turned out to be so successful that it gave the Variety Reduction Program its name.

Organizing a VRP project required putting together an integrated team of designers, production engineers, and consultants. Before embarking upon the VRP project, we asked the team members for some precise answers to the question: "What's wrong with this plant?"

Predictably, no answers were immediately forthcoming. The people who worked in Company A had become so accustomed to the status quo that they were unable to analyze its problems.

Meanwhile, the designer, who had been chosen as project leader, expressed the view that product variety derived from user demand, and that although standardization of parts should be implemented wherever possible, the diversity of remaining parts should be accepted as the inevitable consequence of varying product characteristics. The next test of the project team was to undertake several analyses of diversity. At this point, the project leader found himself stymied by the question of whether or not such variety was inherently necessary. He then accepted the need to return to basics and implement a new analytical approach. Of his own accord he became the project's prime mover.

Dividing its work into several areas of investigation, the project team discovered that the plant had undergone a transformation in the previous five years and offered the following observations:

- The number of basic product types had more than tripled, growing from 4 to 15.
- Sales had tripled.
- The gross value-added rate had decreased by 10 percent.
- The total number of parts distributed within the plant had increased five times.
- The number of assembly lines had tripled.
- The direct labor force had doubled.

In the preceding five years, Company A's sales had definitely grown and the scale of the enterprise had expanded. Nevertheless, its overall performance as represented by profits or value added left a great deal to be desired. In short, the firm's expansion concealed the seeds of unprofitability. Especially damaging was the proliferation of total parts, assembly lines, and workforce. These factors combined to force costs up at a higher rate than the growth in sales.

During those previous five years, the different departments had compensated for deteriorating profits in their own ways. The design department had struggled to speed up new product development; the production technology department had tried to speed up the introduction of high-performance mass production equipment; the production department had secured more storage space to accommodate the growing number of personnel and processes; and the production control department had labored through the introduction of computer systems. The entire company had engaged in a desperate effort to build a box big enough to hold their burgeoning product line and output. What this Pandora's box actually contained, no one really knew until the VRP team was formed.

Cutting Back to Five-Year-Old Levels

The VRP project team set the following target: Except for product variety and sales that could equal or exceed current levels, all figures had to be reduced to the level of five years ago. In other words, the project team would attempt to achieve approximately three times the output of three and a half times as many different products with the same number of parts and production processes used five years earlier. VRP provides the techniques for developing a strategy to minimize parts and processes while responding to market needs and product diversification. This was what Company A needed, and it became the actual goal of the VRP project team.

Obviously, a big difference exists between the approach required to reduce parts or processes by 5 or 10 percent and that required to reduce them by 20 or 50 percent. The former requires the improvement of a few critical points. The latter necessitates a rethinking of the entire production process and a close examination of the fundamentals of product design and production.

Company A's VRP project team took the latter route. They studied the unique features of each product type, analyzed the parts that gave each product its own characteristics, and evaluated the processes by which each part was fabricated and assembled. For every part currently in use, the VRP project team asked the following questions: "What is this part for?" and "Why is this process being used?"

On the basis of this analysis, they adopted these guidelines for developing new products and production systems:

- Adopt design methods treating products as part of a single family instead of as independent units.
- Reduce the number of parts by integrating, combining, and simplifying them as much as possible.
- Set up consolidated product group production lines, integrate and combine processes, and automate as much as possible.

Implementation of the VRP project team's plans began some six months after its initial organization. After one year, although the VRP team had applied its methods to only a portion of the company's product line, it was still able to produce the results shown in Table 2. The number of parts had been reduced by more than half; this decrease had in turn reduced the number of processes by 74 percent — from 461 to 120.

The VRP project team's efforts to reorganize the company to depend on a minimum of parts and processes — even as product variety and sales increased — were a success. Manufacturing costs dropped 30 percent, no small sum. Certainly such a cost reduction would have been improbable by any approach other than VRP. For example, even if the company had cut its factory workforce to zero, production costs would not have been reduced by more than 22 or 23 percent.

• Product–related results			
	Before	After	Avg. change per type
1) Reduction in no. of parts:	90 ➡	40	–55 %
2) Reduction in no. of spot welds:	60 ➡	14	–77
• Process–related results			
1) Reduction in no. of assembly lines:	6 ➡	3	–50
2) Reduction in no. of processes:	–461 ➡	–120	–74
3) Reduction in occupied space:	1500 m2 ➡	860 m2	–57
• Production costs	➡		–30

Table 2: Effects of VRP at Company A

Minimizing Parts and Processes

When the variety of parts used in a plant becomes so great that the company loses track of what is being sent where, trouble lies ahead. (*See* Figure 5.) It is essential for

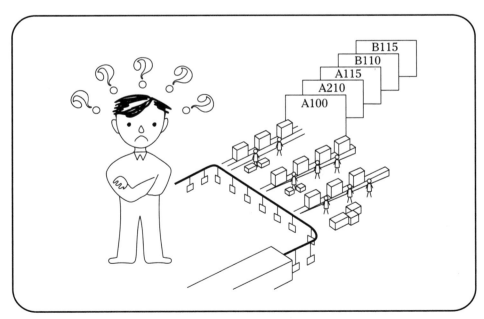

Figure 5: Danger Signal: when products and production processess are no longer comprehensible.

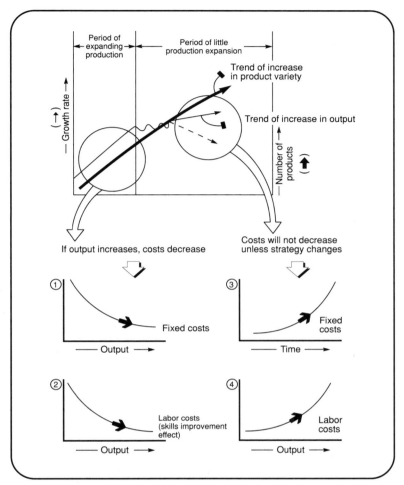

Figure 6: When Product Variety Increases While Output Does Not

managers to recognize that high productivity is impossible in a factory that has lost tolerance for parts diversity. The typical response at best will keep costs from rising but cannot actually reduce them. A company first needs to change its perspective and begin systemic efforts to reduce the variety of parts. Without such a basic understanding of the tolerance levels for parts diversity, it is pointless to clamor for a flexible manufacturing system.

Experience shows that when product variety increase is accompanied by expanding production output, costs drop because the output of each product type increases. Figure 6 illustrates this effect. With expanded output, equipment expenses per product type decrease, labor costs decrease as the mass production effect generates improved skills, and investment in automation equipment appears feasible.

On the other hand, when product variety increases and output grows only slightly or stagnates and declines, costs do not go down. For costs to decrease, a company

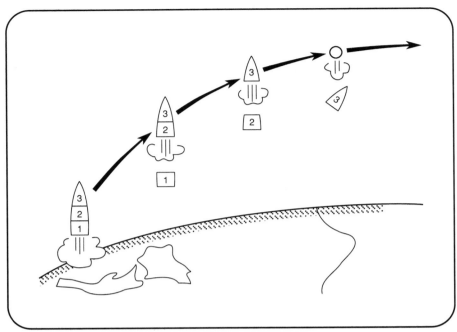

Figure 7: A rocket will not reach outer space unless it lightens its load. A product will not survive in a market unless it is relieved of excess parts and production processes.

must alter its strategy for increasing product variety, producing large quantities of these products and keeping costs low at the same time.

In Company A's case, its delayed strategy resulted in unnecessary grief. Like the rocket in Figure 7 that must jettison successive stages in order to reach outer space, any business must reduce the steps required to design and produce a given quantity of its product as that product comes of age. When a product that has been on the market for three years is still burdened by the same size workforce, the same number of parts and processes, and the same amount of equipment that brought it into the world, that product will not fly for long.

When both the number of products and their output begin a relentless buildup, it is time for a business to reassess what constitutes a reasonable number of parts and production processes. That decision is the key to establishing a strategy that will achieve low-cost production over the long haul.

CHAPTER 2

Reducing Costs in the Midst of Market Diversification

The problem confronted by so many companies is how to stay profitable in the face of demands for product diversification. It is too big an issue to solve by the two methods most commonly used up to now — *standardization* and *value analysis* (VA).

Although companies should persevere in their efforts toward standardization and value analysis, standardization can no longer help respond to market diversification, and VA cannot reduce costs. It is time to ask whether value analysis alone can keep costs down and to examine what cost reduction in the context of increased product variety really means.

Standardization Without Results

Businesses have already devised a number of strategies for dealing with the proliferation of products or parts. One such technique is the process of standardization. Without a standard, the producers and designers of any given product would design and produce it as they liked, resulting in a hodgepodge of products of excessive variety. The remedy has been to set a product standard and require everyone's adherence to it, thereby unifying or consolidating product line and preventing an increase in the number of product types.

Standardization is the process of setting, applying, and managing the implementation of product standards. If the standardization process is applied to parts, then their design and procurement can be expedited simply by referring to the codes for these standard parts.

Management of standard parts differs from management of other parts. A company must check designers' work to ensure that they really do use standard parts as much as possible. Standards need to be set not only in the material realm of actual products and parts, but in the more abstract area of design procedures and related fields. In these areas, the use of standards can eliminate time and energy wasted in solving the same problem twice.

Standards are rules that are set verbally, in writing, or by other graphic means, in the form of models, examples, or other concrete means of expression, to define, specify, and provide detailed descriptions of criteria for measurement, or certain characteristics of units, objects, operations, methods, functions, performance, policy, arrangements, conditions, duties, authority, responsibilities, behavior, attitude, concepts or plans, and ensure their validity for a given period of time.

According to this definition, standardization plays an effective role in industrial development. The process of standardization is a critical undertaking. Unfortunately, most businesses have either reached some ceiling in their efforts to standardize or have not sufficiently incorporated it. For these companies, two major questions may be posed:

1. *Does standardization conflict with technological innovation?*

By articulating and enforcing a fixed standard for a previously disparate group of products, the standardization process gives order to chaos and, by raising the level of technology involved, eliminates errors and redundancy. Further raising or revising of standards provides a solid foundation for systematization, implementation, and subsequent revision. It guarantees the continual advance of standardization. Conversely, continued use of standards set 5, 10, or 20 years ago precludes any progress in standardization. All too often, companies tend to ignore this reality.

2. *Does standardization lead to cost reductions?*

When parts with the same function are used in different types of products, we tend to assume that designing parts to suit each product would be more cost effective than using a standardized part. Cost estimates made at the design stage are often based on two simple factors: (1) the quantity of materials used and (2) the amount of time required for processing and assembly.

Calculating estimated costs from these two factors alone disregards the original objective of standardization, which by definition does not treat products as separate, independent entities. Indeed, the point of standardization is to set a standard for all members of a given product range. Thus, if we look only at one specific product, the use of standard parts might appear to drive material costs higher than would the use of specialized parts unique to that product. By using standard parts for an entire product group, however, both actual material costs and processing costs are lower. In addition, standardization helps reduce overhead costs, treated in cost accounting as fixed costs. In fact, overhead reduction was the reason standardization acquired its reputation as a tool for cost reduction.

Because most businesses habitually err in their estimated costs for individual products, even their designers find it difficult to appreciate the value of standardization. Increasing numbers of product managers have also raised questions about the efficacy of standardization. Only by examining the principles of standardization and applying them carefully can the issues be clarified.

Unfortunately, when it comes to the actual design and development of new products, designers frequently differ from product type to product type. In addition, engineers hate to be accused of imitation. They want to be able to conceptualize freely when they design. While they may appreciate the need for standardization in the abstract, they make no concrete moves in that direction. A company is often left with an empty gesture. Moreover, most design teams are organized by product group, as Figure 8 shows. By definition, such a configuration lacks the perspective required for the horizontal integration of technologies.

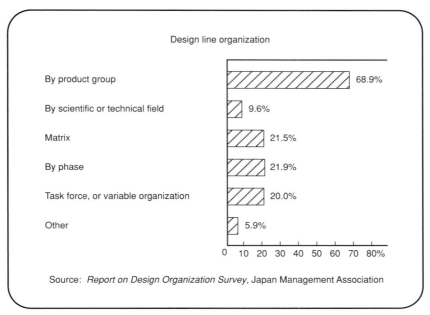

Figure 8: Design by Product Group: Does It Isolate Parts by Product Group?

The introduction of new products results in a lag time and market needs that can yield product differences and hence create product variety.

As Figure 9 illustrates, attempts at standardization vis-à-vis part and process variety cease to be effective when product diversification advances. Lacking a good grasp of the meaning of standardization, companies bury its potential in the proliferation of products, parts, and processes. We need to appreciate not only the basic objectives and effects of standardization but the perspectives and techniques that go beyond it.

How VA Makes Greater Variety Inevitable

Value analysis (VA) attempts to cut costs by defining the value of products or parts by their relationship to function and cost. This idea is expressed in the formula *value = function/cost*.

VA further maintains that *value is the function achieved at the minimum cost*. Thus, VA's first task is to clearly define the function in question. It then considers how to actualize that function at the lowest cost.

Value analysis focuses on isolating the problems associated with products targeted for cost reduction. (*See* Figure 10.) In other words, VA prods researchers to devise

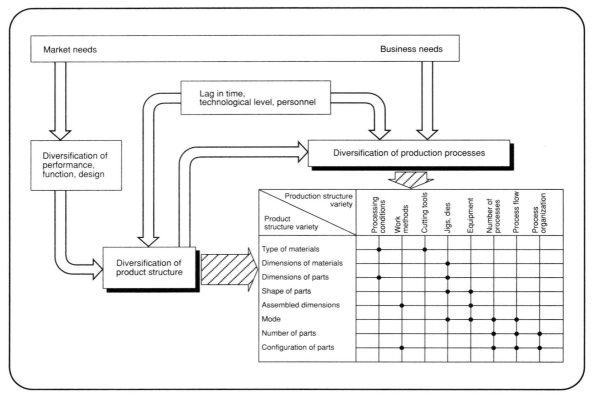

Figure 9: The Causes of Variety Are Not Hard to Find

ways to minimize the cost of any given function by separating it from other functions. Such a research priority is totally incompatible with standardization.

Today, a factory manufacturing only one type of product is rare. It is extremely risky to apply VA to one product or one part at a time. Doing so may indeed show a reduction in the apparent material costs of a single part. When quantities of distinct parts increase, however, the production process grows more complex, resulting in rising processing and overhead costs. The cumulative effect spurs an increase in the number of disparate parts and manufacturing processes. Overall costs expected to go down according to VA calculations actually go up.

A prefabricated structures maker used value analysis to reduce costs. Pushing too hard for the function/cost minimum stipulated by VA, the manufacturer trimmed back each unit's components with the result that every type of unit boasted components with different dimensions. The problem was not evident until the subcontractors manufacturing these units threw up their hands in despair and the manufacturer tried reverting to in-house processing. The magnitude of the blunder then became appallingly clear.

In this case, the manufacturer ignored a cardinal rule of standardization, the rule that made the two-by-four the basis for building construction.

Applying VA may thus exacerbate the increase in parts and processes accompanying product diversification. For many firms it results not in the cost reductions anticipated, but in greater complexity and deterioration of profits.

Another unpleasant consequence of applying VA to individual products while in the midst of diversification is the frequent increase in service parts variety and an unforeseen jump in service costs. The authors do not mean to suggest that the concept of value attained through minimizing costs is useless, but that problems can occur when VA is applied to isolated products in the midst of diversification.

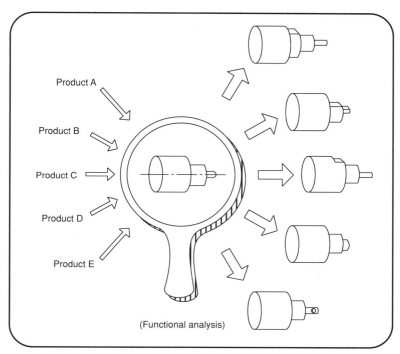

Product A

Product B

Product C

Product D

Product E

(Functional analysis)

Figure 10: Each Product Needs a Slightly Different Part

Functional Costs and Variety Costs

Let's consider two concepts of cost: *functional costs* and *variety costs*. Functional costs are those generated to provide the functions required of a product. Take the fountain pen as an example. To prevent finger slippage to the barrel of a fountain pen, the designers can either attach a part for this purpose or cut notches into the pen's surface. The choice is between a part or a process. The manufacturer incurs the cost of the extra part on the one hand and the cost of the notching process on the other. The manufacturer compares the two and decides on the basis of cost. Figure 11 illustrates how

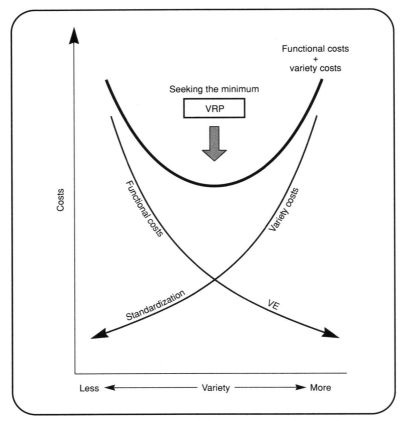

Figure 11: Both Functional Costs and Variety Costs Must Be Reduced

functional costs decline for a large variety of products when reduced in this manner. This cost-reduction process results in the generation of a multitude of different parts. Why? Because the functions required of each product differ. The result gives rise to a second problem known as variety costs.

Variety costs occur when there is a variety of products. Each model of fountain pen requiring completely different parts and processes in turn will require completely different processing equipment. The costs engendered by these differences are variety costs.

We can reduce variety costs by consolidating processing facilities and standardizing parts. Too much standardization, however, creates problems from the standpoint of functional cost containment because of the increasing requirement to use noncustomized parts.

Therefore, functional costs and variety costs are mutually antagonistic. If we pursue a reduction in functional costs for a large number of products, variety costs tend to rise, as shown in Figure 11. By the same token, a reduction in variety costs will be accompanied by rising functional costs. The sum total of both factors is illustrated by a U-shaped curve.

At the bottom of the curve is our goal, the all-important *minimum cost point*. Attainment of this goal requires that we consider how to lower current levels of variety and functional costs.

VRP is the tool by which a company can reduce the sum of "functional costs + variety costs." Extending this concept, we can define functional costs in terms of the actual number of *units* and variety costs in terms of the number of *types* of parts or processes.

The Problem Is the Sum of Types Plus Units

The word *variety* in Variety Reduction Program refers not only to the number of parts or process types but to the sum of the number of types plus the number of component units.

Let's look at parts. When only one product exists, variety refers to the number of part types plus the actual number of part units that comprise that product. When sev-

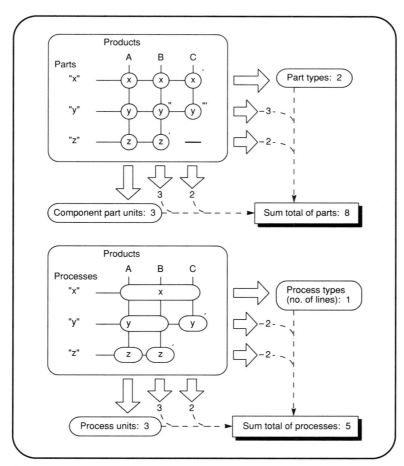

Figure 12: The Problem is the Sum of Types Plus Units

eral products are involved, variety refers to the sum total of part types and part units for each product. In other words, variety, regardless of how many products there are, is the total quantity of parts handled.

The same approach applies to any discussion of processes. When there is only one product, we simply add up the number of different processes — sheeting, welding, painting, assembly, and shipping used to make that product. (VRP does not restrict its definition of processes to the processing and assembly-related operations listed here.) When dealing with a large number of products, we must recognize that different products may require different processes. For example, several types of sheeting processes may be employed, causing the number of process types to increase. Again, variety includes the total number of processes and process types.

The sum of these totals — total parts and total processes — is the focus of VRP. VRP urges us to return to basics by asking key questions. Are these levels high or low? How are they configured? (*See* Figure 12.)

Costs Adhere to Both Parts and Processes

What happens when this sum of parts and processes increases? Based on what we have seen so far, when parts and processes grow, so do a wide variety of expenses. The end result is a factory that is too complex and too costly.

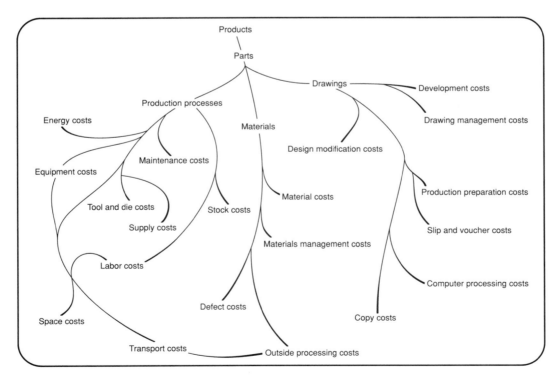

Figure 13: Costs Adhere to Parts and Production Processes

Figure 13 shows that (1) the number of parts increases because the number of products increases and (2) the number of production processes increases because the number of parts and products increases.

1. The amount of equipment increases because the number of production processes increases.
2. Energy consumption increases because the amount of equipment increases.
3. The production workforce increases because processes and equipment increase.
4. The number of drawings, slips, and vouchers increases because the workforce, processes, equipment, and parts increase.
5. Transport increases.
6. Tools and dies increase.
7. Buildings increase.
8. Supplies increase.

Now, we can replace 1 through 8 in the numbered list above with the cost items listed in Table 3. For instance, replace #1 (increased equipment) with Item 14, depreciation expenses, and Item 18, repair expenses. Replace #2 (increased energy consumption) with Item 19, electric power charges, Item 20, gas charges, and Item 21, water charges. Replace #3 (increased production workforce) with Item 3, productive wages,

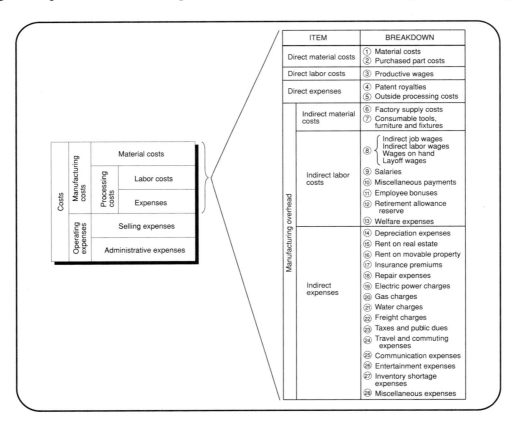

Table 3: Cost Items (Manufacturing Costs)

and Items 8-13, indirect job and labor wages, wages on hand and layoff wages, salaries, miscellaneous payments, bonuses, retirement reserve, and welfare expenses. Replace #4 (increased number of drawings, slips, vouchers) with Item 6, factory supply costs, Item 7, consumable tools, furniture and fixtures, Item 28, miscellaneous expenses, Item 3, and Items 8-13. Replace #5 (increased transport) with Items 8-13, Item 41, occasional direct labor costs, Items 6 and 7, and Item 46, indirect expenses. Replace #6 (growing number of tools and dies) withItems 6 and 7 and Item 14. Replace #7 (building expansion) with Item 15, rent on real estate, Item 17, insurance premiums, and Item 18, repair expenses.

Needless to say, outside processing costs increase along with the growing number of parts. Costs, then, are the accumulation of all the aforementioned items. Cost reduction necessarily entails eliminating the cause of the increase of each item. To do so, we must decide on eliminating, reducing, or changing the character of each cost item implicit in our products, parts, and production processes. Getting back to basics requires questioning the status quo of our parts and processes.

After implementing VRP for a manufacturer of household electric appliances, we wanted to execute a parts management system. Our first step was to analyze costs relating to the production cycle of each part. With a workforce of about 5,000 and annual sales of approximately ¥100 billion ($432,058,760), the appliance company handled approximately 60,000 parts. Parts-related management costs in all departments ranging from design to service totaled ¥360 million ($1,555,411).

On an average, each part cost the company about ¥60,000 ($259). This amount included expenses incurred once a month and recurrent expenses. Under the new parts management system, this total was unacceptably high.

The magnitude of the influence of parts' quantity levels on costs should be evident by now (*See* Figure 14). When a business asks itself what to do about the level of total parts or processes it employs, it has taken the first step toward solving its problems.

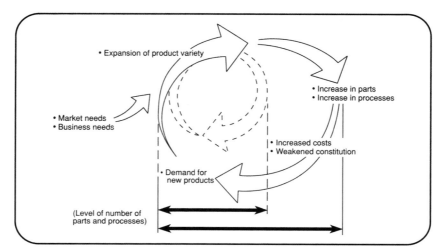

Figure 14: The Level of Parts and Processes Determines the Constitution of a Business

CHAPTER 3

The VRP Approach

The Variety Reduction Program's approach is to provide products that meet diversifying market needs while also reducing the number of required parts and production processes. Consequently, VRP includes methods called "Making Highly Profitable Plants" and "Lowering Product Costs Everywhere from Products to Production."

From Type Y to Type X

Looking at any one product, we can predict that the number of product types or models will gradually increase as its market expands. The total number of component parts and processes will generally grow in proportion to the increase in product types. Until now, this formula has been taken for granted — within a few years of new product introduction, the number of different models and component parts is expected to multiply.

Designers, production engineers, all production-related departments, and eventually the entire operation get caught up in the struggle to support an ever more complex product line. To make matters worse, even when the product reaches the end of its life cycle and sales start falling off, the company will be unable to halt this proliferation of product types. Instead, it will try to cover sales losses by tossing one new product after another into the ring, thus compounding the problem. Eventually, this unhappy firm will plunge into a sea of red ink.

Figure 15 provides us with a graphic depiction of this pattern. Since it resembles the letter *Y*, we call it Type Y. VRP tries to convert Type Y into a Type-X pattern, in which product types increase with market changes but total number of component parts and processes does not increase at the same rate. Furthermore, the rate of increase in parts and processes peaks at the beginning and gradually declines thereafter.

A Type-X business structure is the goal of VRP. Put another way, our goal is a structure that allows no deterioration in profitability throughout the life of a product. To achieve a Type-X structure, a business must be able to answer the following questions:

- What characteristics and market niche does each product in the product group possess?
- How many parts are used to provide the characteristics of each product?
- How many processes are used to produce each product at the required output?

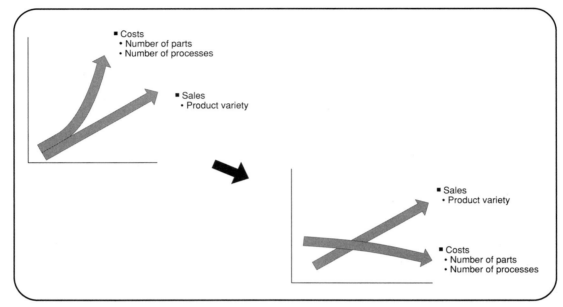

Figure 15: From Type Y to Type X

Finally, the company must deal with the level of parts and processes as a single yardstick in its analysis.

Reducing V, F, and C Costs

Generally, we calculate costs using the formula *total costs = materials costs + number of processes × processing costs.* Design engineers use this formula when making cost estimates during the product design stage. Accordingly, they do not stop to think of other possible costs. In reality, however, use of this formula to calculate all costs is dangerous for several reasons:

1. In many cases, the category of material costs means the cost of materials at the time they are delivered to the plant by outside suppliers. No one knows how much of these costs are taken up by the supplier's processing costs.
2. Often, people calculate the number of processes simply on the basis of parts produced to go into the products. As we noted earlier, such thinking based on parts production does not work in this era of wide variety and numerous parts. In other

much. In reality, however, these costs will fluctuate if improvements are made that actually change the process equipment. Thus, designers generally fail to account for improvements that can influence processing costs.

In view of these factors, an alternative means of calculating costs is needed.

In VRP, we instead use the formula *total costs = V costs + F costs + C costs*. This formula lets us probe much deeper to reveal hitherto overlooked cost factors. This same VRP method helps reduce the number of parts and processes.

One factor that leads to expansion in the volume of parts and production processes is the sheer variety of such parts and processes. In fact, the cost incurred by such variety is proportionate to the range of variety. This cost is the V (Variety) cost discussed in Chapter 2. V costs do not arise from individual products or processes but rather from multiple models or types.

Also contributing to the proliferation of parts and processes is the number of individual parts and processes. The cost incurred by this factor is the F (Function) cost, also introduced in Chapter 2. The form — and even the existence — of such parts and processes depend upon the product specifications, designed functions, and product construction method. All these factors contribute to the F cost and cause it to fluctuate.

The cost incurred by the people in the design, production technology, materials, and production departments is known as the C (Control) cost. Consequently, the C cost is higher in companies that develop many different products and must therefore manufacture a wide variety of products or in companies that are contracted to design and manufacture products. Even if two companies have equal product development costs, their C costs may vary depending upon their component parts, production processes, and the nature of their outside supplier relationships.

Figure 16 shows how VRP relates these VFC costs to all processes and reduces cost.

The V Cost Approach

The V cost can be broken down into two categories. Figure 17 shows one category, *type-related costs,* which are costs arising from the variety of part types and production process types. These costs include expenses for retooling, new dies and equipment, and other investment costs incurred when producing a new type of part. In the past, many companies have tried to promote flexible production by fitting production equipment to produce a wide variety of parts. When the variety of these companies' parts overtaxed the versatility of their production equipment, their response was to retool the equipment. Next, when the assortment of types grew even larger, they had to give up on the old equipment altogether and invest in new equipment. It was the same story for their dies. The moral is that companies can reduce the number of processes and assembly labor hours by continuing the same or similar work operations for large

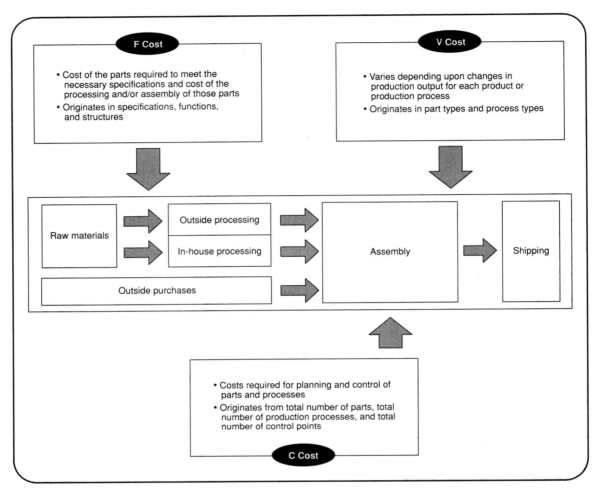

Figure 16: F Cost, V Cost, and C Cost

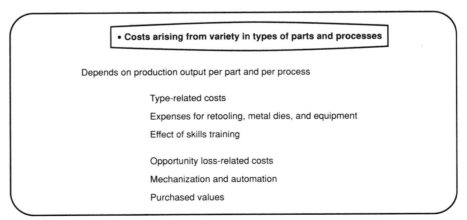

Figure 17: The V Cost Approach

quantities of workpieces. Conversely, a greater variety of work operations means more labor hours and higher costs. All such costs arise directly from the variety of parts produced.

The other V cost category is *opportunity loss-related costs.* Such costs occur in companies that have work operations suitable for mechanization or automation but have not been able to invest in such systems because of the diverse array of parts being produced. The loss of opportunity for money-saving investment incurs a cost. Moreover, the diversity of parts forces companies to set prices without fully studying purchased values, which also drives up costs.

"Production output per part" and "production output per process"

Figure 18 illustrates how costs change depending on two vital factors: "production output per part" and "production output per process."

Even assuming a fixed production output for overall products, the production output per part shrinks as the variety of parts expands. Conversely, more standardized parts means a greater production output per part. As shown in the figure, the cost levels change accordingly.

The greater the quantity of parts produced by a single production process, the lower the cost level. To increase the output of parts per process, we must make the production processes more flexible while also increasing similarity in processing and assembly specifications among different part types.

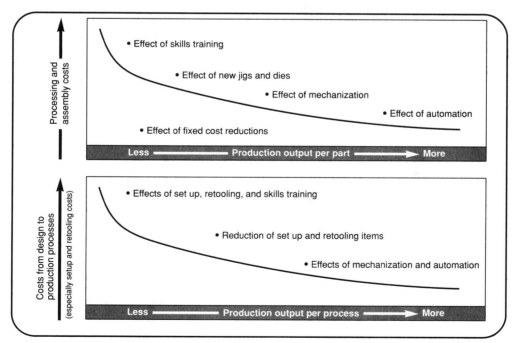

Figure 18: Two Vital Cost Factors: "Production Output per Part" and "Production Output per Process"

The F Cost Approach

Decisions concerning product specifications and structural designs are based on market and client needs. In concrete terms, product structures are collections of parts, and a different production process is required to make each of the product's parts.

If we look closely at the overall process by which raw materials are processed, assembled, and shipped by these individual production processes, we notice materials, equipment, and work operations. The raw materials move from one process to the next until the desired part or product is completed.

As shown in Figure 19, the materials used in individual production processes can be seen as the "materials cost," while the equipment and work operations can be looked at as the "processing cost" and "assembly cost." We can refer to the collective costs thus generated as the F cost.

The F cost depends heavily on how well market needs and client needs are translated into product structure. It also depends on the system used to produce the product. Since production includes inspection and packaging, the costs related to these processes are also part of the F cost.

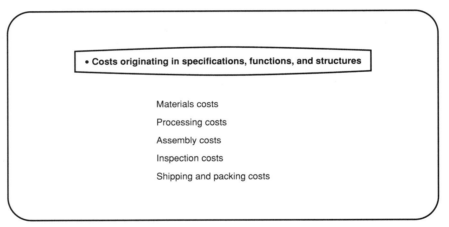

Figure 19: The F Cost Approach

The C Cost Approach

The C cost can be readily understood if we follow the flow of the drawings (and drawing data) generated in the design department and the flow of the materials and parts that enter the plant. After being drafted by the design department, drawings that concern internally produced items go mainly to the production technology department, where they are used in preparing the required equipment, jigs, and tools as well as in writing the work instructions that are passed to the production department. This flow of events incurs planning and control costs.

Meanwhile, the materials and/or parts that enter the plant are initially warehoused and later supplied either to the various processes or directly to the production processes. In either case, control costs related to inspection, quality control, and other control procedures are incurred.

Characteristically, this C cost level rises as the amount of newly designed parts increases and as the volume of subcontracted and delivered parts expands. In Figure 20, the C cost is shown to consist mainly of "information" generation costs, labor costs related to conveyance and control of parts and/or materials, and equipment costs tied to planning and control.

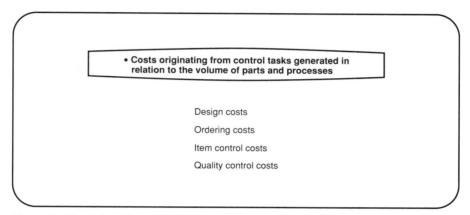

• Costs originating from control tasks generated in relation to the volume of parts and processes

Design costs

Ordering costs

Item control costs

Quality control costs

Figure 20: The C Cost Approach

What is the C cost for one drawing?

Market production companies have a harder time grasping C costs because they generally are not in the habit of keeping track of personnel costs in management and related departments on a per-drawing or even a per-product basis. On the other hand, companies that design and produce on a contract (order-specific) basis do tend to monitor their design labor hours and other management labor hours for each project; thus they are in a better position to understand C cost accounting.

In either case, all companies employ some customary yardstick for measuring costs. Contracting design and production companies tend to group costs around individual projects, while market production companies tend to group costs in units of months or "terms." The important thing is what the resulting cost figures are used for. The cost accounting should be geared toward the use of the cost data. Since the purpose of C cost accounting is to reduce costs, cost data are grouped around things such as drawings, parts, and control points. To be exact, they are grouped around the control points pertaining to the drawings and parts.

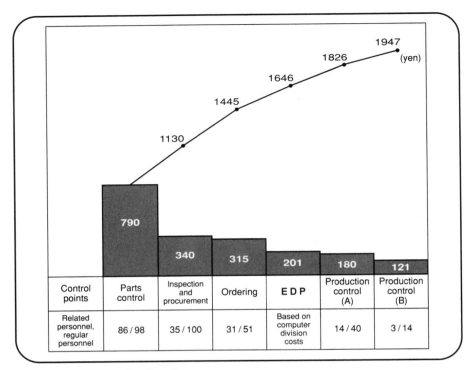

Figure 21: C Cost for One Drawing

Figure 21 shows an example of C cost accounting targeted at a single drawing. There are six control points for this drawing, and costs have been figured for each.

Splitting the Pie Among the V Cost, F Cost, and C Cost

In the past, the F cost has often accounted for more than 90 percent of overall costs. In today's companies, however, the product diversification trend is widening the V cost and C cost shares of the pie. In mass production industries such as the automotive and consumer electronics industries, the F cost often accounts for between 50 percent and 70 percent of overall costs, while the V cost ranges from 20 to 30 percent and the C cost from 10 to 30 percent. In special-order industries such as heavy electrical equipment, the F cost ranges from 40 to 60 percent of total costs while the V cost takes up 20 to 30 percent and the C cost 30 to 40 percent. (*See* Figure 22.)

Integrated Industrialization

We use the word *industrialization* to mean the development and manufacture of products. The definition includes product planning, design, production preparation,

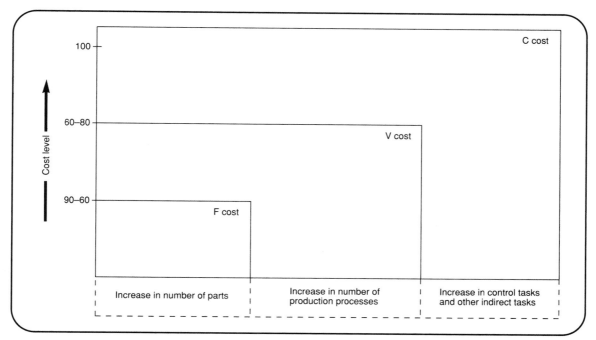

Figure 22: Shares of Total Cost Held by V Cost, F Cost, and C Cost

and production itself. VRP, then, is a program for this larger concept of industrialization.

We take a certain product group and define each of the products composing it. We next apply VRP's five concepts to the structures of these products and production systems to reduce the level of parts and processes. Finally, we prepare for implementation, then actually implement and follow up. Following these steps is like descending a spiral staircase, as indicated by Figure 23. While the characteristics peculiar to a given product or enterprise will dictate certain additional actions besides the ones listed here, these basic activities will still exhibit this spiral pattern of industrialization.

Another key aspect of VRP is project organization. As work progresses, the personnel involved may increase or the allotment of tasks may change. The spiral on the right in Figure 23 represents the steps involved in project organization. VRP deals simultaneously with product groups and process groups, and hence it requires teamwork by everyone involved in marketing, design, production technology, and manufacture.

VRP advances these dual processes of action and project organization in order to maximize current operation and future effectiveness. When consulting on VRP for European and American companies, we often hear comments such as, "VRP is integrated industrialization, isn't it?" In terms of how a VRP project advances, this is certainly an accurate observation. VRP is not merely a means of improving parts and processes to reduce costs, however. It is a series of activities from development to

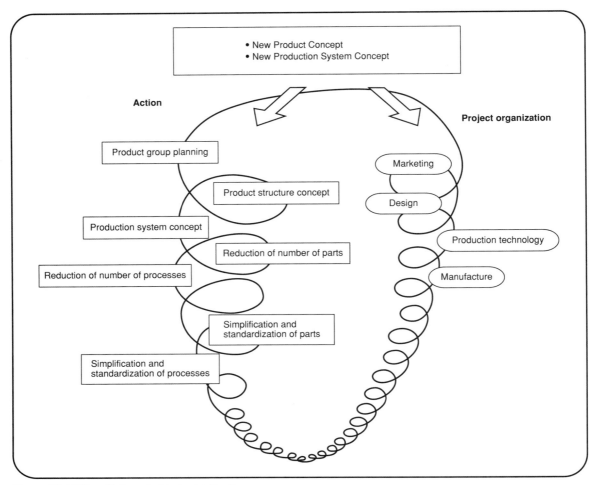

Figure 23: VRP as "Integrated Industrialization

execution — it selects a certain group of products and processes, sets up a project to formulate a new generation of products and production systems, and then puts that plan into effect. VRP is a program that can create an entirely new structure for an enterprise.

It is also a technique for bringing a business's engineers and managers together to create new products. Our clients in the United States and Europe frequently told us that the use of integrated technical/managerial organization must surely be the reason Japanese businesses do so well. To be honest, we wonder how many Japanese firms really grasp the significance of such an organization. Our country, too, has barely scratched the surface in this regard.

PART II

VRP Methods

Variety Reduction Program (VRP) requires that we articulate not only the current character of our products, parts, and processes but the concepts according to which this character will change. This section explains the techniques VRP uses for this purpose.

CHAPTER 4

VRP Indices for Cost Reduction

Analysis and Evaluation of VRP Indices for VFC Cost Reduction

VRP includes the evaluation of VRP indices. Incremental progress in driving down costs for the group of targeted products helps lower the VRP indices, and the result is not only lower product costs but also a comprehensive firming up of the organizational structure. As such, the evaluation of VRP indices constitutes a basic VRP activity.

Accordingly, when evaluating VRP's cost-cutting effect on the product group, we look for lower percentages in manufacturing costs as well as a downtrend in the VRP indices themselves.

As shown in Figure 24, the VRP indices consist of the parts index, production process index, and the control point index. These indices serve to indicate how well a company's plant is performing in developing and manufacturing products. The parts index and process index can show significantly different figures for two plants even when they are turning out the same product. The better company is that which can develop and manufacture the product using fewer parts and fewer production processes. When these indices show a sudden rise from the previous year or the year

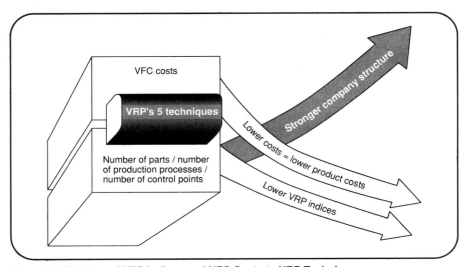

Figure 24: Relation of VRP Indices and VFC Costs to VRP Techniques

before that, they serve as a warning that the company is moving toward a high-cost organizational structure.

Are the VRP Indices Going Higher?

Figure 25 illustrates how the VRP parts index is calculated as the product of the number of parts times the number of part types that go into a particular product. Likewise, the production process index indicates how many lines and how many processes use a particular part or product; it is the product of the number of lines or production sites times the number of processes. The control point index is based on the number of control points, wherein each substantial change in the control process relating to the flow of drawings and the flow of materials and parts is counted as one control point.

The first thing we look for is a rising trend in the VRP indices. If they are rising, then we check for a conspicuous increase in new parts. Next, we carefully analyze whether the causes for the increase are the only factors involved in reducing the VRP indices. After analyzing the rate of increase for each index and the various causes, we can discover factors that characterize the types of product development and profitability that exist at the factory concerned. Once we understand the factory's characteristics through VRP index analysis, we are ready to plan for lowering the VRP indices to strengthen the factory's organizational structure. We can, for example, set a goal of halving the parts index and draft a plan of activities to achieve that goal.

Case Study: An Increase in Parts and Production Processes

Let's consider a case in which a company purchases three types of automobile windshield wipers (small, medium, and large) from a parts shop. Using VRP techniques, we analyze the number of constituent parts and production processes that have gone into the making of these windshield wipers to derive a cost-accounting basis. These VRP techniques enable us to see just how easily the number of parts and processes can and do increase.

Figure 26 shows the results of a VRP analysis of these windshield wipers.

In this case, the VRP parts index — in other words, the number of parts times the number of part types — is 925. In turn, the VRP production process index — the number of processes times the number of working assembly lines — is 399. Here we see how a windshield wiper that comes in only three types can generate rather large VRP index values. Imagine the kind of index values that result when there are several dozen types! In fact, many actual VRP projects to date have involved VRP index values on the order of seven- or eight-digit figures. And each one of these VRP index points contributes to overall costs.

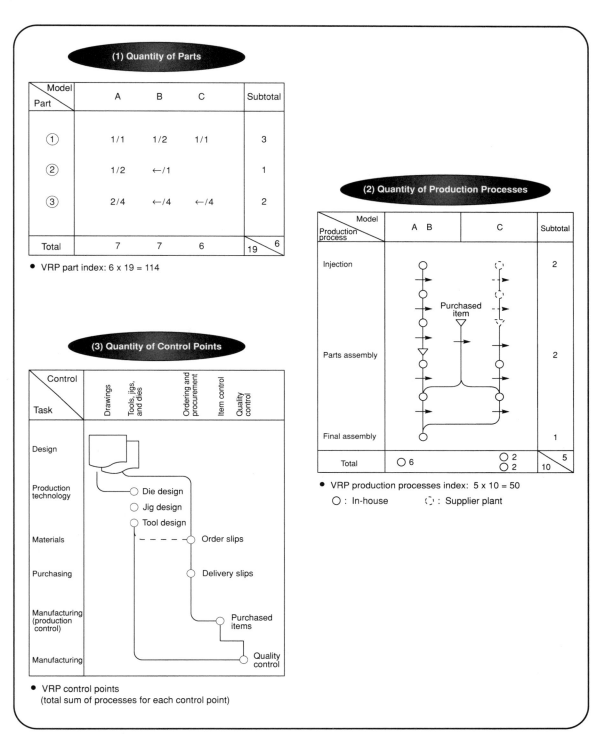

Figure 25: Are the VRP Indices Going Higher?

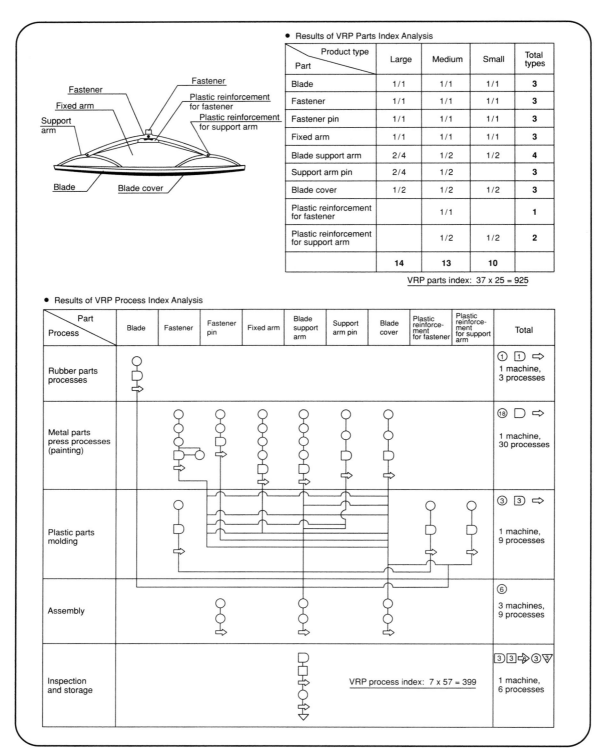

Results of VRP Parts Index Analysis

Part \ Product type	Large	Medium	Small	Total types
Blade	1/1	1/1	1/1	3
Fastener	1/1	1/1	1/1	3
Fastener pin	1/1	1/1	1/1	3
Fixed arm	1/1	1/1	1/1	3
Blade support arm	2/4	1/2	1/2	4
Support arm pin	2/4	1/2		3
Blade cover	1/2	1/2	1/2	3
Plastic reinforcement for fastener		1/1		1
Plastic reinforcement for support arm		1/2	1/2	2
	14	13	10	

VRP parts index: 37 x 25 = 925

Results of VRP Process Index Analysis

Part \ Process	Blade	Fastener	Fastener pin	Fixed arm	Blade support arm	Support arm pin	Blade cover	Plastic reinforcement for fastener	Plastic reinforcement for support arm	Total
Rubber parts processes										1 machine, 3 processes
Metal parts press processes (painting)										1 machine, 30 processes
Plastic parts molding										1 machine, 9 processes
Assembly										3 machines, 9 processes
Inspection and storage										1 machine, 6 processes

VRP process index: 7 x 57 = 399

Figure 26: Case Study

Lowering VRP Indices and Cutting Manufacturing Costs

Figure 27 shows a graph that plots the relationship between:

1. the parts index and production process index and
2. manufacturing cost figures taken from the results of a VRP project.

As can be seen in the figure, a 50 percent cut in the two VRP indices corresponds to a roughly 30 percent reduction in manufacturing costs.

Some companies have worked for years to lower their VRP indices. In such companies, a 50 percent drop in the VRP parts index and a 30 percent decrease in the production process index is no small feat. In many cases, three years of sustained cost-cutting efforts resulted in VRP index reductions ranging from 10 to 20 percent. One might think that reducing manufacturing costs by 30 percent would be impossible for such companies, but it is quite possible if the companies rethink their entire approach toward parts and production processes.

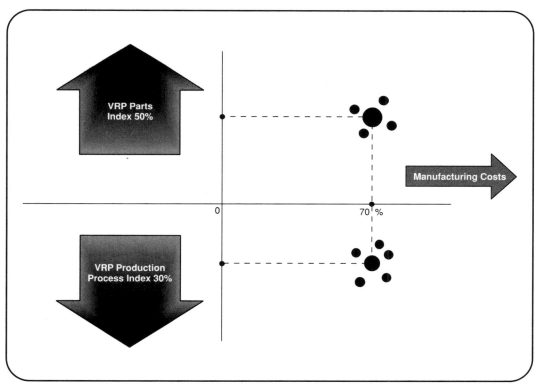

Figure 27: 50 Percent Lower VRP Indices Means 30 Percent Lower Manufacturing Costs

Therefore, the statistics plotted in Figure 27 should be considered the initial results of cost-cutting efforts at a company that has not yet begun to implement VRP activities aimed at halving parts costs.

Configuration of VRP's Five Techniques

Figure 28 shows the configuration of VRP's five techniques:

1. *fixed vs. variable*
2. *combination*
3. *multifunctionality and integration*
4. *trend*
5. *range*

In a company whose VFC cost levels are high, we can expect to see a great number of control points for its currently used parts and production processes. We can also expect to find a complicated array of parts and production processes and a wide variety of dimensional values, including many size specifications that are difficult to meet. As this company attempts to reduce costs, it must ask itself:

1. how to view the structures of its products and production system
2. where to begin using the cost-cutting ax
3. how to lower its VRP indices
4. how to establish a lower cost level.

Figure 29 illustrates such a company's product and production structures. Here, we are using the *fixed vs. variable* and *combination* techniques to change the *configuration method* employed for the parts and production processes. Meanwhile, we use the *multifunctionality and integration* technique to simplify and optimize the systems and specifications. Finally, we use the *trend* and *range* techniques as the most suitable techniques for establishing dimensional and volume values that incur minimal costs.

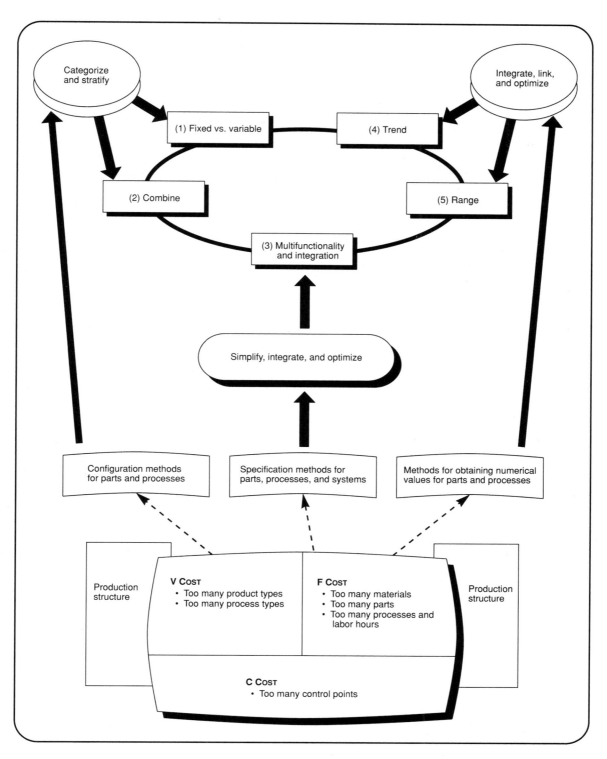

Figure 28: Configuration of VRP's Five Techniques

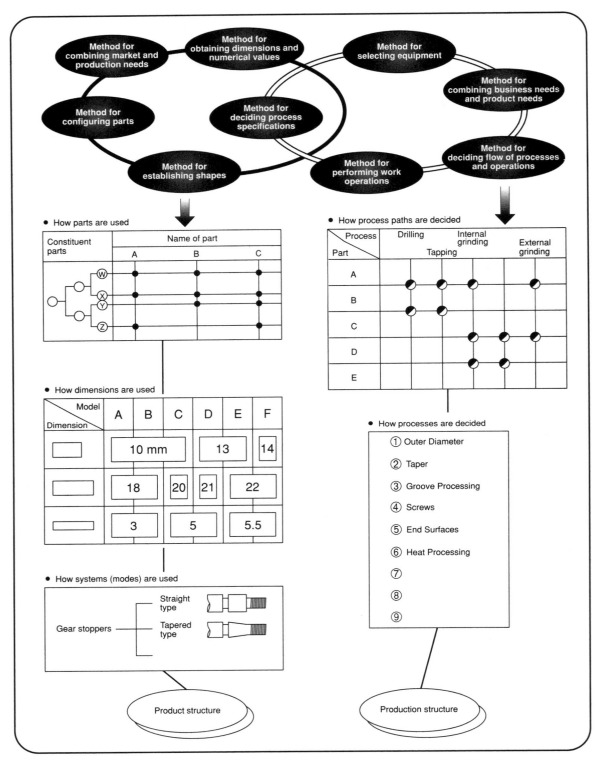

Figure 29: Parts and Production Process Indices

Using VRP's Five Techniques to Design for Lower VFC Costs

Although we can use VRP's five techniques for cutting VFC costs, we must first discover the different characteristics of each of these costs. Then we must apply the five techniques of VRP in a manner that is appropriate for those characteristics.

Figure 30 shows how the *multifunctionality and integration* technique can be used to reduce the F cost. The figure also shows how the *fixed vs. variable* technique can be applied for cutting the V cost and how the two techniques together can help lower the C cost. Meanwhile, we use the *trend* and "range" techniques for overall VFC cost slashing.

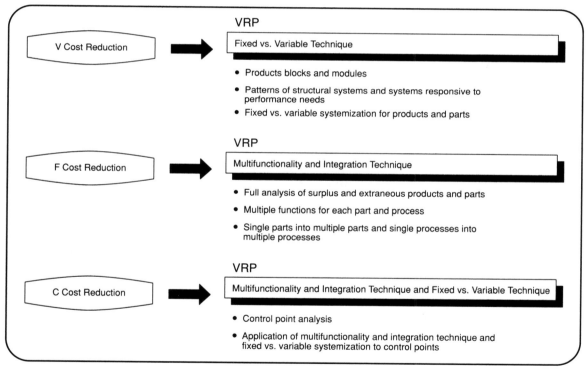

Figure 30: Using the Five Techniques of VRP to Cut VFC Costs

Product Structure Analysis

Before getting into the five techniques of VRP, we should carefully examine the product and production structures. A full understanding of these structures is necessary because the five techniques of VRP entail an overhaul of their designs.

Let's look first at product structures. Figure 31 shows the product example we used earlier, namely, a set of automobile windshield wipers. These windshield wipers seem very simple at first glance, but since they have to fit a variety of automobiles and must operate well under all driving conditions, they must be designed to meet a wide range of functional requirements and other needs.

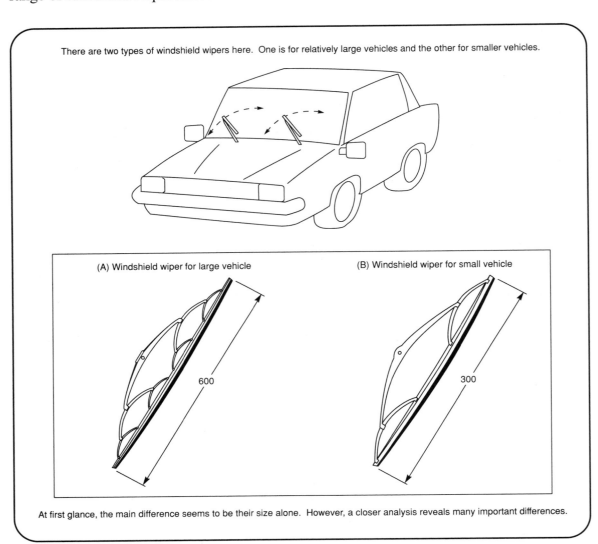

There are two types of windshield wipers here. One is for relatively large vehicles and the other for smaller vehicles.

(A) Windshield wiper for large vehicle

(B) Windshield wiper for small vehicle

600

300

At first glance, the main difference seems to be their size alone. However, a closer analysis reveals many important differences.

Figure 31: Product Structure Example: Windshield Wipers

Numerical value, systems and specifications, and configuration methods for establishing new product structure

Numerical values, systems and specifications, and *configuration* are the three elements we use in establishing a new product structure. These elements give rise to various parts, which in turn come together as individual products. Figure 32 illustrates this product structuring process, which includes several parts levels. Some simpler products require fewer levels than are shown in the figure.

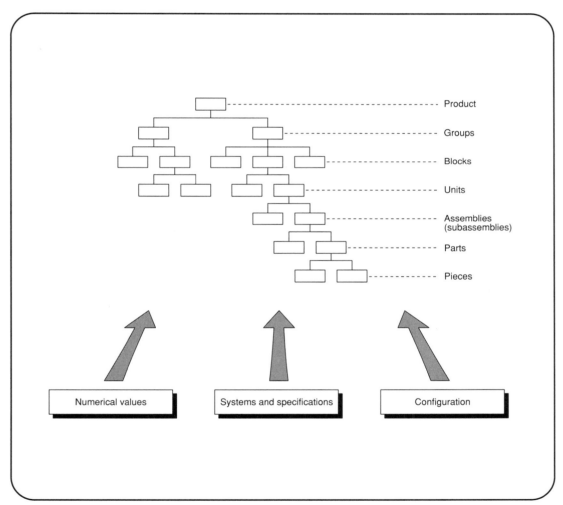

Figure 32: Product Structure Levels

Numerical values

In product structures, we use numerical values to indicate a product's performance and characteristics as well as its shape and size. Product performance and characteristics are generally indicated in the product specifications. In this instance, we are speaking of *numerical values* strictly with regard to a product's shape and size. Figure 33 shows the system of numerical values for our example of automobile windshield wipers.

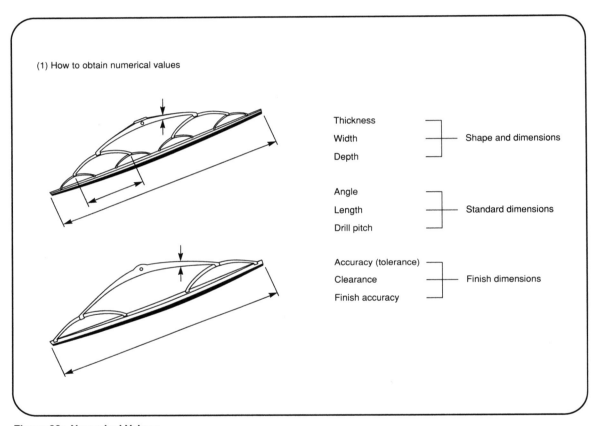

Figure 33: Numerical Values

Systems and specifications

By *systems* we mean the procedures and methods used to realize the desired functions and performance features in a product. Even when the product's functions precisely meet the needs sought in the product, there are still many ways in which the product's structure can be different. Naturally, we often design such *systems* simply to make the product more *distinctive*.

By *specifications* we mean the numerical values and design concepts that are expressed as product characteristics and performance features or as its design requirements. We elucidate these specifications as product requirements when dreaming up product systems.

Figure 34 shows how systems and specifications come into play in our example of auto windshield wipers.

These systems and specifications form the backbone of the product structure, so we need to know which particular systems and specifications to use. In other words, we need to seek the systems and specifications that produce the desired effect in the product to satisfy market and/or client needs.

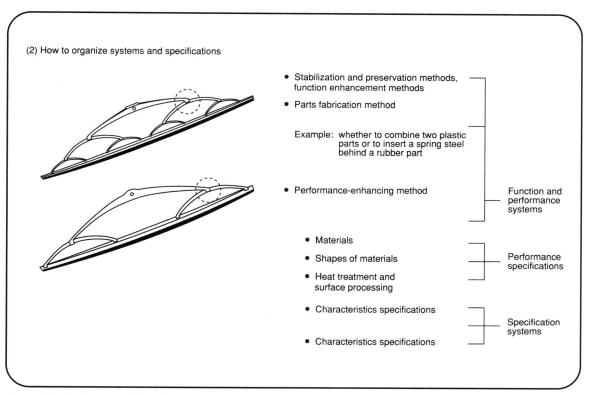

Figure 34: Systems and Specifications

Configuration

By *configuration* we mean the method we use to combine the parts that make up the product in question.

As shown in Figure 35, we use different configurations for the small and large windshield wipers. The small windshield wiper consists of two subassemblies, while the large windshield wiper includes three subassemblies plus one other part. In this case, the small windshield wiper is configured as a windshield contact subassembly and a wiper arm subassembly, and we can simply combine these two finished subassemblies to make the product.

If we look at a wide assortment of automobile models, we can see quite a variety of windshield wiper part configurations. This diversity has a major impact on production process organization. This impact is felt most strongly in the assembly processes.

In some cases, we use the same combination of parts but a different parts layout. If the parts layout differs, the assembly processes must differ to some degree, and this will produce various effects on peripheral parts as well.

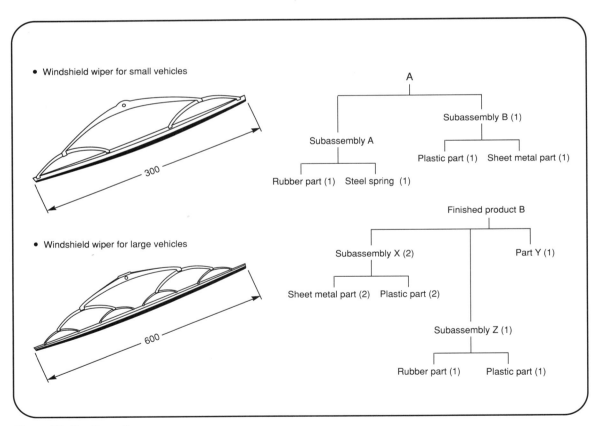

Figure 35: Configuration

Causes for Greater Variety in Product Structures

As we saw earlier, we establish a product's variety (*i.e.* , its number of parts and VFC cost factors) by the different numerical values, systems and specifications, and configurations employed for each product. Product structure variety also increases easily when we establish various methods for making the products. Figure 36 lists some of the reasons for this:

```
[1] Different client (market) needs

[2] Different design periods

[3] Different designers

[4] Different design concepts

[5] Different design methods

[6] Different production technologies
```

Figure 36: Causes for Variety in Product Structures

Production Structure Analysis

Production processes differ greatly depending upon whether they are for processing or for assembly, that is, whether their function is to make parts or to combine them. As shown in Figure 37, product assembly processes can include several levels and depend very much upon the choice of product configuration method.

Another key factor in determining the production process format is whether the production process is located in-house or at an outside supplier. We must also remember not to confuse production processes with work operations, since they are substantially different. Production processes consist of the elements shown in the figure, and their basic function is to take a part in the process of changing raw materials into finished products. By contrast, work operations are single jobs performed by a person or machine at a particular stage in the production process.

Process paths, processes, processing and assembly elements, and operation points

We can delineate several elements in the relation between production processes and product structure, namely process paths, processes, processing and assembly elements, and operation points. These elements are shown in Figure 38.

• Process paths arise from the different product models or part types, and their patterns can grow larger when adopting a different production process flow, which also raises costs. In other words, the variety of production process increases, causing a corresponding rise in costs for equipment, dies, jigs and tools, and so on.

- As parts or processes become more complicated, more production processes are needed to produce the required shapes and sizes. This is another cost-boosting factor.
- Processing and assembly elements are the most numerous when several part types are processed and/or assembled as part of a single production process.
- Operation points are activities that must be done by a machine or a human operator. We count operation points as the number of turns of a screw, number of spot welds, and the like. The higher such numbers go, the higher the related cost rises.

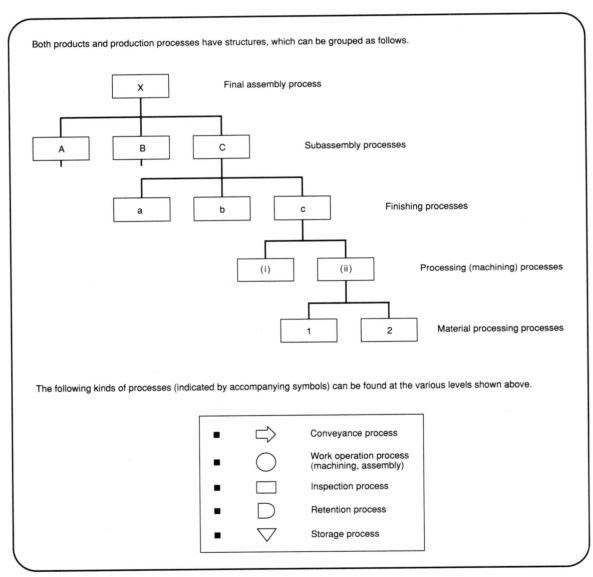

Figure 37: Production Structure

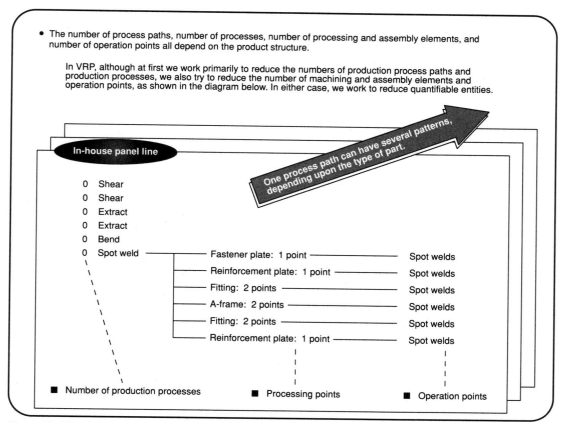

- The number of process paths, number of processes, number of processing and assembly elements, and number of operation points all depend on the product structure.

  In VRP, although at first we work primarily to reduce the numbers of production process paths and production processes, we also try to reduce the number of machining and assembly elements and operation points, as shown in the diagram below. In either case, we work to reduce quantifiable entities.

In-house panel line

One process path can have several patterns, depending upon the type of part.

0 Shear
0 Shear
0 Extract
0 Extract
0 Bend
0 Spot weld ——┬—— Fastener plate: 1 point ——————— Spot welds
              ├—— Reinforcement plate: 1 point ——— Spot welds
              ├—— Fitting: 2 points ——————————— Spot welds
              ├—— A-frame: 2 points ——————————— Spot welds
              ├—— Fitting: 2 points ——————————— Spot welds
              └—— Reinforcement plate: 1 point ——— Spot welds

■ Number of production processes   ■ Processing points   ■ Operation points

Figure 38: Elements in the Relation between Production Processes and Product Structures.

A change in the product structure means a change in the production structure

Product structure and *production structure* are closely interrelated.

Product structure changes according to the production output, equipment design concepts, production control method, and so on. Changes in *production structure*, on the other hand, are more fundamentally determined by changes in the product structure. As shown in Figure 39, such things as "process paths" and "production processes" are determined by product elements, including "numerical values" and "systems and specifications."

We have seen how product structures and production structures both comprise many elements and how they relate to each other. The way in which these constituent elements are combined can make the difference between high and low costs.

Figure 40 shows how various causes can lead to greater variety in product structure and production structure. In VRP, we analyze these causes, then use the five techniques of VRP to minimize diversification of parts and production processes even as the products become more diverse, and to come up with structural designs that reduce the number of required parts and production processes.

Product Structure \ Production Structure	Process path	Process	Machining and assembly elements	Operation points	Operations		Equipment	Dies, jigs, and tools
					Adjustment	Retooling		
Numerical values		✳		✳	✳	✳	✳	✳
Systems and specifications	✳	✳	✳	✳	✳	✳	✳	✳
Configuration	✳	✳	✳	✳	✳		✳	

Note: Asterisks indicate major impact

- The following can be said of the windshield wiper example.

  - The materials are the same but the shapes are different. . . . The dies are different or the machining centers are different (additional types of processes).

  - One type uses plastic and rubber, while the other uses a spring steel and rubber. . . . Subassembly processes are different (additional types of processes).

  - One type uses plastic caulking, and the other uses only a gripfastener. . . . Additional caulking processes

  - One type includes 14 parts while the other has only 5 parts. . . . Additional assembly processes

Figure 39: Product Structure and Production Structure

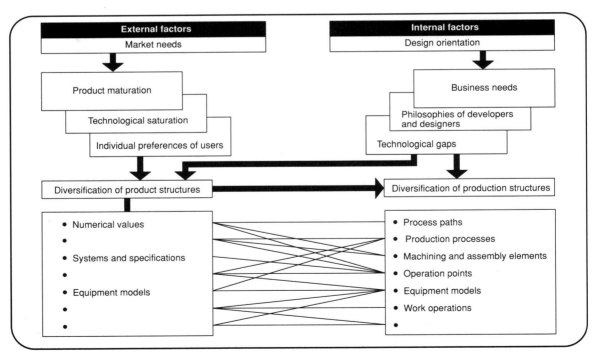

Figure 40: Diversification of Product Structure and Production Structure

CHAPTER 5

The Five Techniques of VRP

VRP Technique 1

VRP Technique 1 is called *fixed vs. variable*. We can apply this technique in determining a product structure's *numerical values* and *configuration* as well as in setting up *process paths* and equipment or die structures.

For each product, we establish fixed parts as standard, commonly used parts to meet the functional needs of a variety of models, parts, and processes, and we establish its variable parts as the parts that actively address changing market needs. This enables us to keep the variety of parts and production processes to a minimum even amidst product diversification. Once we have completed this categorization, we establish a system for implementing thoroughgoing rationalization of all fixed parts while vigorously seeking to ensure profitable variety in variable parts. In the past, many companies have pursued a lopsided approach in which they sought extreme variability in parts and products while seeking stability in rationalization of production and greater design efficiency. The overall effect of such an orientation has generally been a major loss in profitability.

Figure 41 illustrates the *fixed vs. variable* technique.

Design of fixed vs. variable product/production systems

As shown in Figure 42, even the equipment and jigs used in production processes can be designed as fixed parts in relation to the product. Since fixed parts require a relatively smaller range of specifications, they are conducive to the promotion of mechanization and automation in the interest of higher production output. As for variable parts, it is important to plan sophisticated systems for operation control themes such as a supply system geared toward a broad specification range and a large quantity of parts. Examples of such systems include automatic parts reception and supply systems and VAN systems for sending instructions to operators and outside suppliers.

Such systems, in which we clearly distinguish between fixed parts and variable parts and establish a system to address each type of part, are called *fixed vs. variable product/production systems*.

The fixed vs. variable technique

As shown in Figure 43 (page 60), the fixed vs. variable technique consists of (1) an analysis of the relation between market needs and product structure, (2) proposals for increasing the number of fixed parts by studying possible fixed parts, and (3) proposals for a fixed vs. variable system.

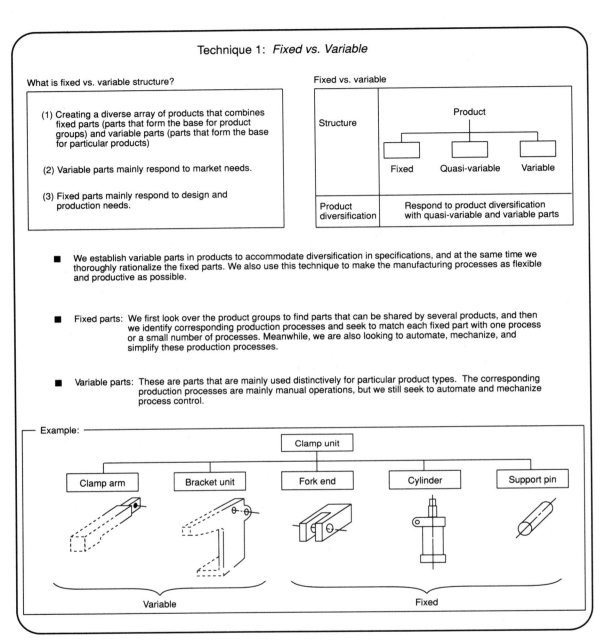

Technique 1: *Fixed vs. Variable*

What is fixed vs. variable structure?

(1) Creating a diverse array of products that combines fixed parts (parts that form the base for product groups) and variable parts (parts that form the base for particular products)

(2) Variable parts mainly respond to market needs.

(3) Fixed parts mainly respond to design and production needs.

Fixed vs. variable

Structure	Product: Fixed, Quasi-variable, Variable
Product diversification	Respond to product diversification with quasi-variable and variable parts

■ We establish variable parts in products to accommodate diversification in specifications, and at the same time we thoroughly rationalize the fixed parts. We also use this technique to make the manufacturing processes as flexible and productive as possible.

■ Fixed parts: We first look over the product groups to find parts that can be shared by several products, and then we identify corresponding production processes and seek to match each fixed part with one process or a small number of processes. Meanwhile, we are also looking to automate, mechanize, and simplify these production processes.

■ Variable parts: These are parts that are mainly used distinctively for particular product types. The corresponding production processes are mainly manual operations, but we still seek to automate and mechanize process control.

Example:

Clamp unit — Clamp arm, Bracket unit, Fork end, Cylinder, Support pin

Variable: Clamp arm, Bracket unit
Fixed: Fork end, Cylinder, Support pin

Figure 41: Fixed vs. Variable

Production process \ Product		Fixed	Quasi-variable	Variable
		Units A & B	Units C & D	Parts E, F, & G
Fixed	Line **A**	■ Standardization ■ Mechanization ■ Automation		■ Diverse types ■ Manual operations
Quasi-variable	**B**		■ Patterning ■ Flexible mechanization and automation	
Variable	**C**	■ Mixed-flow processes ■ Product groups, mechanization, and automation		■ Diversification, wider array of types ■ More advanced control methods

Figure 42: Design of a Fixed vs. Variable Product/Production System

VRP Technique 2

The second VRP technique is called combination. Like the fixed vs. variable technique, the combination technique is a means of dealing with diversification.

Combination means clearly delineating product functions for each parts-combination unit that goes into products.

Two good examples of this technique are the BBS (Building Block System) for machine tools and the modularization of toys and other products. Figure 44 (page 61) illustrates the combination technique.

Design of combination product and production systems

Applying the combination method to products is premised upon the design of standardized units and parts. This allows for the reduction of variety in parts and process or assembly systems.

A production system that is designed to turn out products made with the combination technique is the foundation for efficient production of standardized units and parts.

As for contracting design and production companies, they can also devise a system for keeping costs to a minimum, as shown in Figure 45 (page 60). We call this kind of system a combination product and production system.

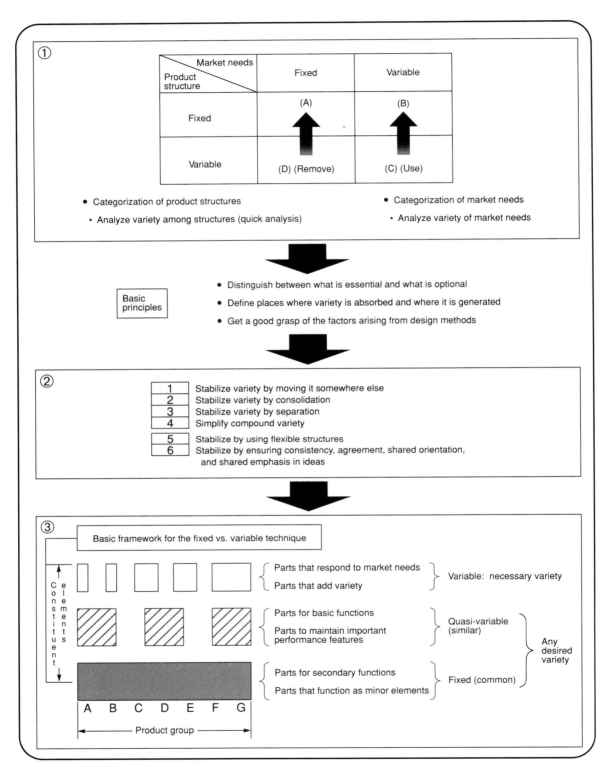

Figure 43: The Fixed vs. Variable Technique

Combination Technique

Combination

Structure	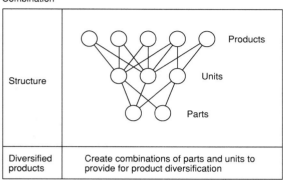 Products Units Parts
Diversified products	Create combinations of parts and units to provide for product diversification

- Combination:
  To simplify the array of products and remove gaps between product features and needs, we simplify parts and units and try to create combinations of exchangeable parts and units to provide for product diversification.

What is a combined structure?

(1) Blocks and units must be exchangeable

(2) Blocks and units must be amenable to upgrading and downgrading

(3) Must be able to create a wide array of finished products simply by interchanging blocks and units

(4) Must be able to combine blocks and units in ways that meet market needs

Example:

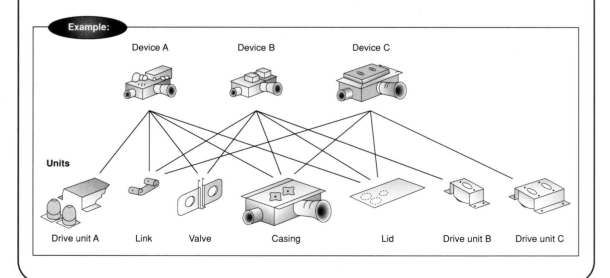

Figure 44: The Combination Technique

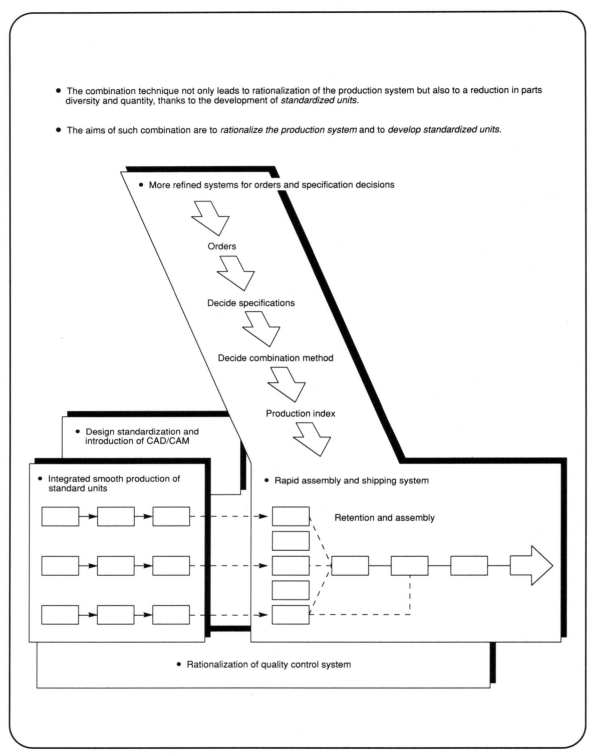

- The combination technique not only leads to rationalization of the production system but also to a reduction in parts diversity and quantity, thanks to the development of *standardized units*.

- The aims of such combination are to *rationalize the production system* and to *develop standardized units*.

- More refined systems for orders and specification decisions

  Orders

  Decide specifications

  Decide combination method

  Production index

- Design standardization and introduction of CAD/CAM

- Integrated smooth production of standard units

- Rapid assembly and shipping system

  Retention and assembly

- Rationalization of quality control system

Figure 45: The Combination Product and Production System

We use the following techniques, which are illustrated in Figure 46, to find out how to apply the combination approach.

1. *Base plus augmentation technique.* We first establish the basic parts among the products and production processes, such as basic structural parts and added parts. Then we make various combinations of the added parts to create a variety of finished products.
2. *Identical module combination technique.* We first establish identical modules, and, in principle, make all of our products just by varying the number of these modules.
3. *Independent module combination technique.* In this case, we combine different kinds of modules, each designed for specific functions, to make the products.

We can apply the combination technique not only with parts and units themselves but also with standard dimensions and functions.

The combination technique means that even when changes have been made in design specifications, the structure of the units need not change. Design changes will be met simply by introducing new combinations. In combining these units, the key is to maximize standardization and modularization by avoiding the use of specialized parts and by minimizing the number of parts that must be screwed on or soldered together.

VRP Technique 3

The third VRP technique is called multifunctionality and integration. In contrast to the first two VRP techniques, which seek to minimize the variety (and therefore the *V* cost) of parts, process paths, production processes, equipment, and dies in response to diversification in products and specifications, *multifunctionality and integration* seeks to reduce the numbers of constituent parts in each product and the number of production processes for each product to minimize the F cost.

As shown in Figure 47, *multifunctionality* means to look at products from the perspective of functions and to build a product structure that includes only the minimum amount of parts required to fulfill the desired function. *Integration* means that even when the numbers of parts and functions have been minimized, we employ new materials, production technologies, or structural concepts to integrate the required functions into a fewer number of parts.

We begin by studying both *multifunctionality* and *integration*, which enable us to reduce the numbers of parts and production processes. Reducing the number of parts must come first, setting the stage for a streamlining of production processes.

- There are many combination methods; which one to use depends on the target product or production characteristic. Combination techniques can also be used jointly with the fixed vs. variable technique.

Various Combination Methods

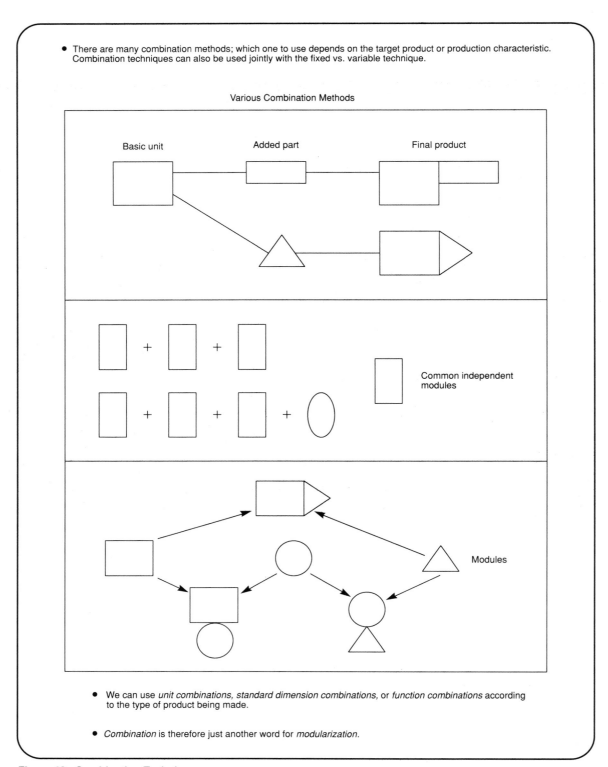

- We can use *unit combinations, standard dimension combinations,* or *function combinations* according to the type of product being made.

- *Combination* is therefore just another word for *modularization.*

Figure 46: Combination Techniques

Technique 3: *Multifunctionality and Integration*

The purpose of this technique is to create a structure that provides the desired functions using only a minimum of parts and having a very simple design, thereby reducing the number of parts and production processes required.

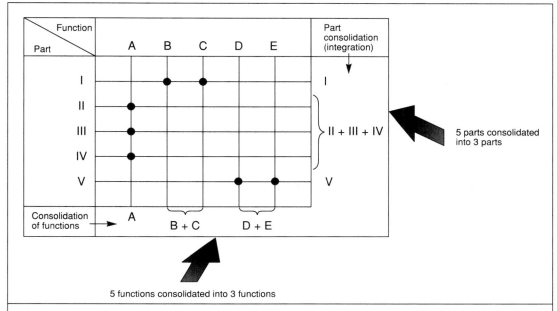

5 parts consolidated into 3 parts

5 functions consolidated into 3 functions

Set up the product to include a minimum of functions and parts. Set up the production system to include a minimum of processes.

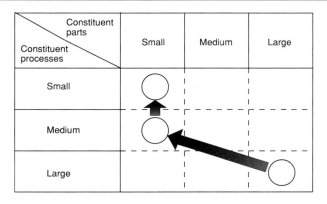

Figure 47: Multifunctionality and Integration

Studying multifunctionality and integration

Figure 48 is a description of the main techniques used to study multifunctionality and integration. We begin drafting proposals for structures that require fewer parts and production processes. These proposals refer to functions and structures using words such as *remove, combine, replace,* and *new system.* In studying functions, we must begin with specifications and then proceed to functions, parts, and production processes, in that order.

	Remove	Combine	Replace	New System
Functions (Specifications)	• Remove "surplus" specifications and functions that are not absolutely needed for the particular needs and objectives	• Integrate multiple functions into a single part or process	• Replace with something else	• Propose a new system or set of specifications
(Functions)		• Combine functions		• Simplify and streamline
Structure (Parts)	• Remove "surplus" procedures that are not absolutely needed for the particular needs and objectives	• Integrate parts and production processes • Combine parts and production processes	• Replace with something else	• Propose a new system or set of techniques
(Production processes)				• Simplify and streamline

Figure 48: Multifunctionality and Integration Techniques

VRP Technique 4

The fourth VRP technique is called *range.* Etymologically, *range* is derived from words meaning "to arrange," "to line up," and to "classify." We apply this technique mainly when working with elements such as dimensions, numerical values, and specifications. We analyze them to find a *width* or *range* within which a particular dimension, numerical value, or specification value can be applied and then use these *ranges* to minimize costs.

Taking the example of a part's dimensions (shown in Figure 49), we try to create a dimension that will be applicable in as many models as possible.

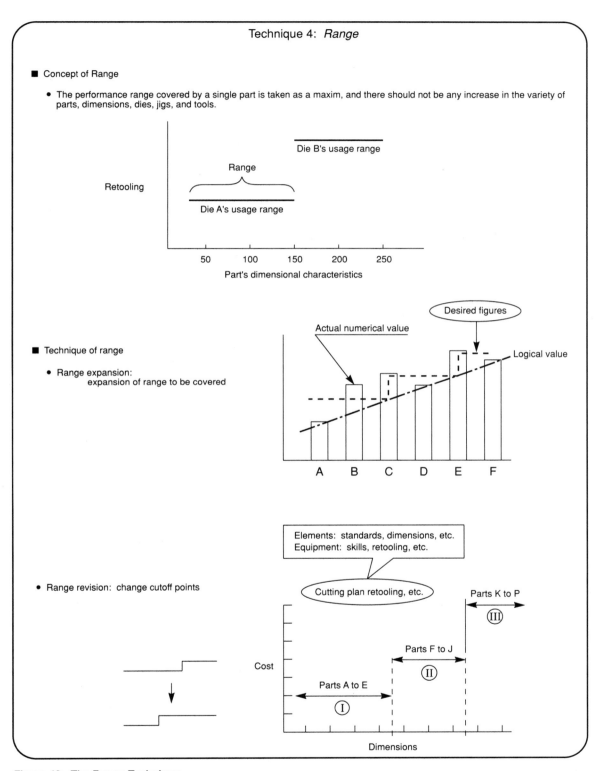

Technique 4: *Range*

■ Concept of Range

• The performance range covered by a single part is taken as a maxim, and there should not be any increase in the variety of parts, dimensions, dies, jigs, and tools.

Die B's usage range

Range

Retooling

Die A's usage range

50   100   150   200   250

Part's dimensional characteristics

Desired figures

Actual numerical value

Logical value

■ Technique of range

• Range expansion: expansion of range to be covered

A   B   C   D   E   F

Elements: standards, dimensions, etc.
Equipment: skills, retooling, etc.

• Range revision: change cutoff points

Cutting plan retooling, etc.

Parts K to P

(III)

Cost

Parts F to J

(II)

Parts A to E

(I)

Dimensions

Figure 49: The Range Technique

Even when it comes to the dies used in production, we should change the production system so that instead of designing new dies to retool for new models, we need only replace certain parts of the dies to obtain the required die dimensions and structures, thereby eliminating unnecessary variety. Our study of the range technique is broken down into a study of ways to expand and otherwise change the application range of values of structures.

VRP Technique 5

The fifth technique is called *trend*, or the organization of measured values into statistical trends. This technique determines whether the measured values have any ordering principle.

Usually, when we have looked closely at the numerical and specification values that are generated by diversification, we have been able to identify an ordering principle by which we can establish a trend. We are thus able to reduce cost factors and eliminate the generation of unnecessary parts, production processes, equipment, and die retooling operations.

As shown in Figure 50, our study of trends is centered on analyses of the manner in which variation occurs and of the characteristics of cost generation. In the latter analysis, we try to find out what effect specific variations have on certain parts and production processes.

Figure 51 illustrates an example of such a trend study.

Technique 5: *Trends*

(1) We use this technique to apply a single consistent principle in managing the performance and function features required in production equipment and parts. We do the same in revising dimensional values or specifications.

(2) To do this, we plot variations as a trend. For example, we can decide to consistently take the geometrical mean or the arithmetic mean of the performance-related numerical values or the dimensional value. This is useful when standardizing equipment specifications or production conditions such as fastening torque and axial width, or fastening torque and rotational speed.

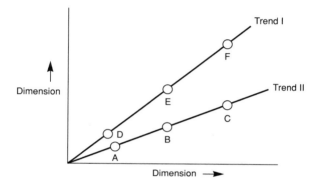

■ The trend technique

  ● Plot variations as numerical trends

  ● Take the geometric mean or arithmetic mean of the performance-related numerical values

  ● Take the geometric mean or arithmetic mean of the dimensional values

Figure 50: The Trend Technique

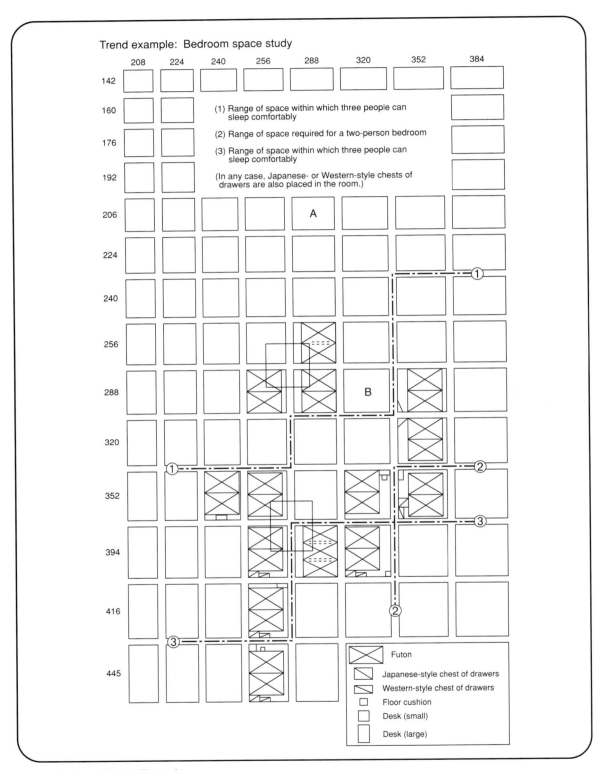

Figure 51: Trend Study Example

PART III

VRP's Advancement

When implementing VRP, it is important to recognize the program not merely as a method of developing products and production systems with few parts and processes, but as a means of achieving integrated industrialization and as a product cost reduction design method. VRP coordinates the work of people from different departments as they follow a series of steps from the design through the actual creation of new products and systems. In most cases to date, product development that previously took two or three years was reduced by VRP to only a year or year and a half. These results are mainly due to VRP's distinctive application of a number of coordinated techniques to products organized in groups.

CHAPTER 6

VRP Project Planning

Project Planning

The basic principle of any comprehensive cost reduction project using VRP techniques is to direct cost-cutting activities toward every single source of costs. Accordingly, every department that has any relation to the target group of products should participate in the project.

Such broad-based efforts are easily hampered, however, by outdated statistics concerning the target product group and by the diversity of opinions about the product group held in–house. In addition, the various departments are often busy with their own problems and daily tasks. In such a situation, a company must have the strong support of top management, which means a clear company wide message from top management affirming the project's importance and necessity, as well as a clear indication of the project's direction.

The project planning stage is thus a crucial stage indeed, and one that must be seen to completion before taking any steps to implement the project. Figure 52 describes some of the items that must be addressed during the project planning stage.

Setting Specific Goals

As shown in Figure 53, the values we set as goals can be expressed in many different ways, depending upon the conditions placed on the product group. In any case, we must set specific, clearly defined goals. We must also be clear about the project's scope, setting goals not only for a rate of cost reduction but also for an absolute-value cost reduction goal.

Often, however, people establish their target values before broadly analyzing the current situation, and instead base their targets on some vague idea of what is necessary or what would be a fairly difficult goal to reach. Consequently, many people set a cost reduction rate target of between 20 and 30 percent.

By contrast, in the VRP approach to cost reduction we deal directly with the cost generating factors — namely, the overall parts index and the number of processes — and set target values in these categories as specific goals for our cost-cutting activities.

Generally speaking, a 20 to 30 percent cost reduction rate requires a 50 percent reduction in overall parts index and a 30 percent cut in the number of processes, which obviously entails some major changes in products and processes.

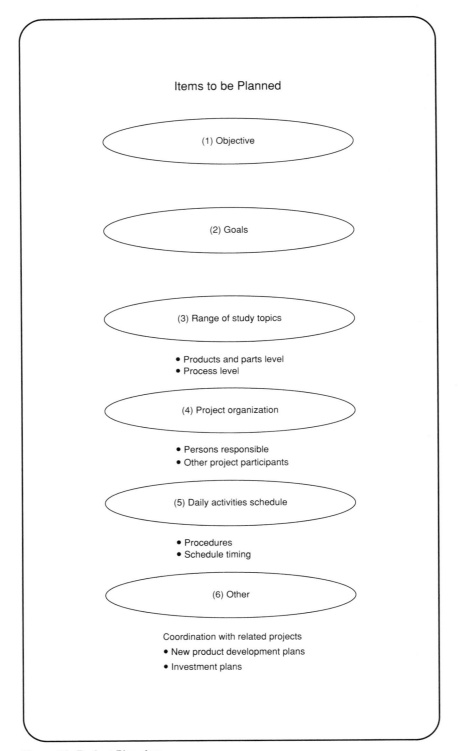

Figure 52: Project Planning

In setting these targets for success, we must never forget to clearly state the benchmark time.

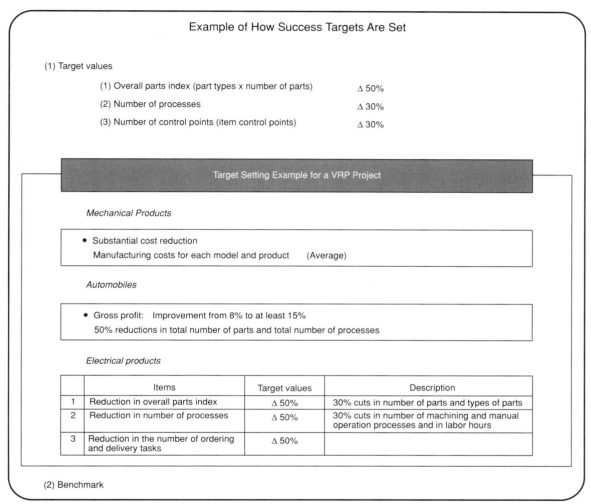

Figure 53: Success Targets

Setting the Scope of Studies

In VRP, we focus on product groups. In other words, instead of looking at one particular model, we direct our cost-cutting activities toward several. Consequently, we must first select the models to include in the product group. Naturally, there are times when we might need to target all of the models, but generally it is wiser to restrict the scope of VRP activities by considering matters such as the products' expected position a few years from now, the relation between basic models and other models, technological innovation trends, and market trends. Such a restricted focus helps make the project's activities more efficient.

It is also sometimes helpful to restrict the focus beyond product units and instead work at the device unit level.

Some groups carry out concentrated cost-cutting activities focused upon device units that are significant in terms of cost and/or technology, while other groups work the opposite way by first excluding items that do not suit the project activities.

Similarly, when it comes to production processes, we basically target all of the processes, but we also tend to concentrate on those which are most significant in terms of cost and/or production technology. In addition to the company's own processes, we also select explicit targets at suppliers either at the company level or at the process level, so that VRP activities can address needs for process improvements at those suppliers. (*See* Figure 54.)

In any case, there must be a definite scope within which we can set and attain our VRP goals.

Makeup of Project Team

Since the project teams are the nucleus of VRP activities, their configuration is obviously a very important matter. Figure 55 shows how these project teams are organized and the roles their members play.

Optimally, the executives in charge of the targeted product groups should also be the people responsible for organizing the project teams. These executives should oversee the creation of two organizations, the project team itself and an in-depth study group.

The project team takes charge of the various project tasks; its members handle matters such as design, production technology, manufacturing, materials, sales, marketing, and cost control. Among these member assignments, those covering design, production technology, and manufacturing are further broken down into specialist member assignments covering specific projects on separate production lines. The other, nonspecialist members take on various other assignments. The number of members shown in Figure 55 is the minimum number, and this number changes depending on the details of the project. Basically, though, there must be a balance among the target values, the project period, and the number of project team members.

As for the in-depth study group, they first meet at the project conceptualization stage, digesting all the ideas proposed by people in the various related divisions. Each meeting is actually a two-day seminar, in which the study group members make an in-depth analysis of the themes established by people from various company divisions. Generally, they hold from four to six of these seminars over the course of a project.

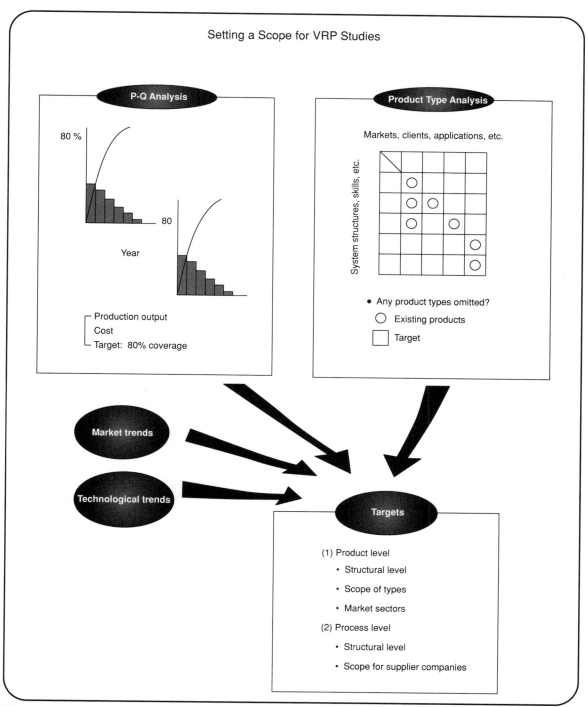

Figure 54: Scope of Targets

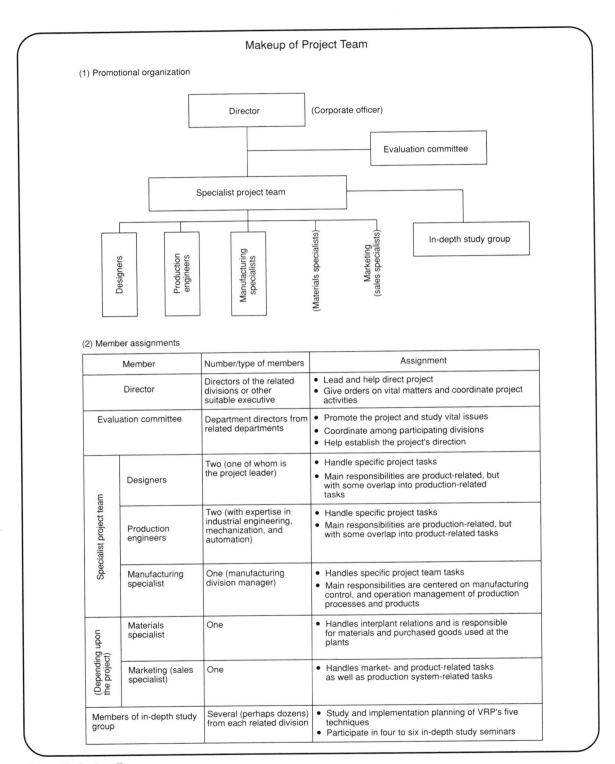

Figure 55: Project Team

Creation of A Daily Activities Schedule

We set up a daily activities schedule as a means of scheduling projects into major steps and of recording authorization for each step. We obviously use the project period as the basic framework of such a schedule, but we must also take pains to coordinate the various internal periods, such as for product development planning, business planning, and investment budgeting. Basically, we should try to coordinate and link the schedule with the product development cycle.

Activity periods vary according to the characteristics of the targeted product group, but we can generally say that if the product cycle is one year, the project conceptualization stage must end within four to six months in order to be coordinated with the product cycle.

This daily schedule should also include the scheduling of evaluation committee meetings and in-depth study group seminars. The seminars should be scheduled as early on as possible, since so many people from so many divisions are involved, and this requires a lot of interdepartmental planning and communication.

It is best to set up the special task schedules within each project step about once a month, as the project proceeds.

Figure 56 shows an example of a daily activities schedule.

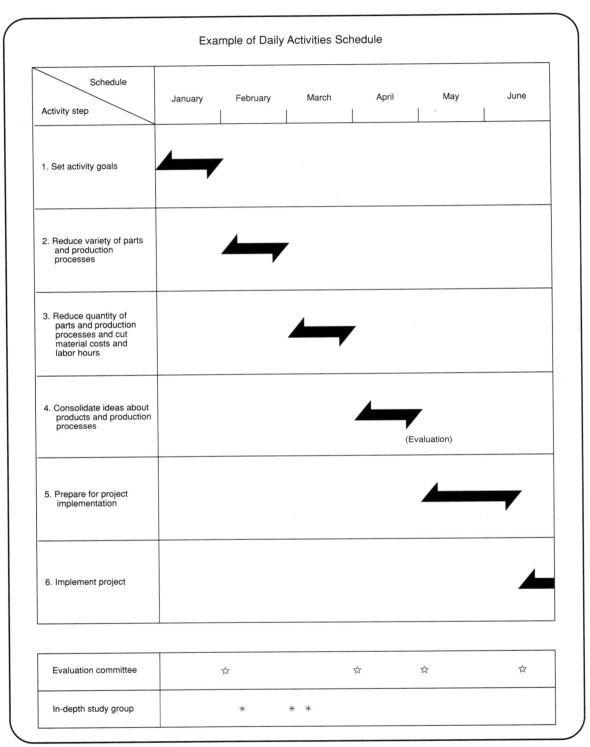

Figure 56: Daily Activities Schedule

CHAPTER 7

How to Develop VRP Projects

There are seven basic steps to follow in VRP project development. However, this can change depending on such factors as the project theme, goals, target products, and production conditions.

VRP project development steps

Figure 57 describes the seven basic steps used in VRP project development.

In step 1, we seek to grasp current conditions regarding costs, parts, and production processes and to clarify what must be done to reduce costs. We also break down the target goals into specific goals for each unit and cost item, and then begin establishing concrete activity goals.

In steps 2, 3, and 4, the project team proposes ideas for bringing down costs. These steps form the core of the VRP project and are where we put VRP's five techniques to work. During this period, members of the related divisions also hold in-depth study seminars.

In step 5, we compile and evaluate the ideas resulting from the brainstorming and in-depth studies. In steps 6 and 7, we begin implementing the ideas that were evaluated and approved in step 5. Now we should begin thinking about expanding the VRP promotional organization. Even after implementation has begun, the project team must keep tabs on how the implementation is proceeding and help the organization to promptly respond to any problems that arise.

Naturally, the activities during these two steps vary greatly depending upon the character of the project, the points emphasized, and other incidental details.

Analysis of Product Group Characteristics

When studying cost-cutting proposals, we sometimes need to clarify the characteristics of the target product group and the issues that are likely to arise as we pursue our VRP goals. Even two companies that produce the exact same product will have different characteristics, different problems, and different proposals simply because they are different companies.

We can examine these characteristics from various perspectives, including "market position," "the product development situation," "profit conditions," and "the production system." As shown in Figure 58, the VRP analysis in which we come from each of these perspectives to grasp the product group's characteristics can be called

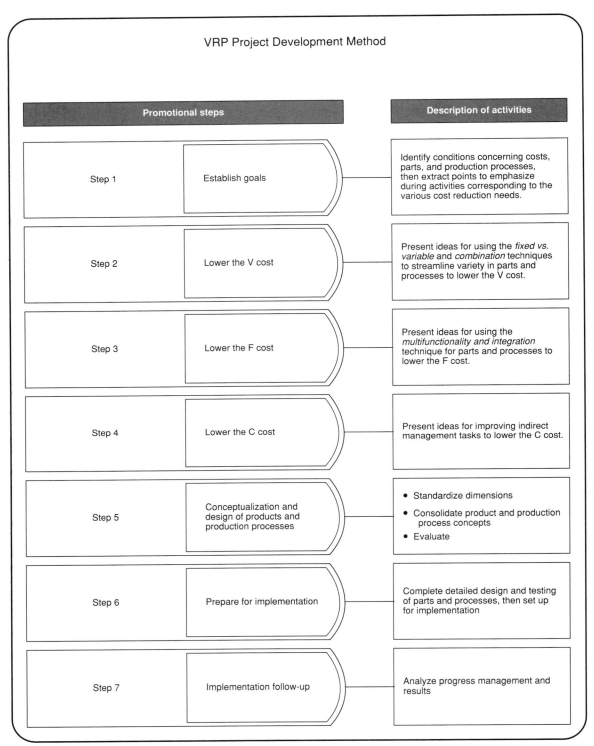

Figure 57: The Seven Steps of a VRP Project

"market position analysis," "product history analysis," "profit position analysis," and "production system history analysis." If we can clarify our intentions and targets based on such analyses, we can then take on issues such as "market related issues," "product development issues," "profitability issues," and "production rationalization issues" in a way that suits the product group's characteristics.

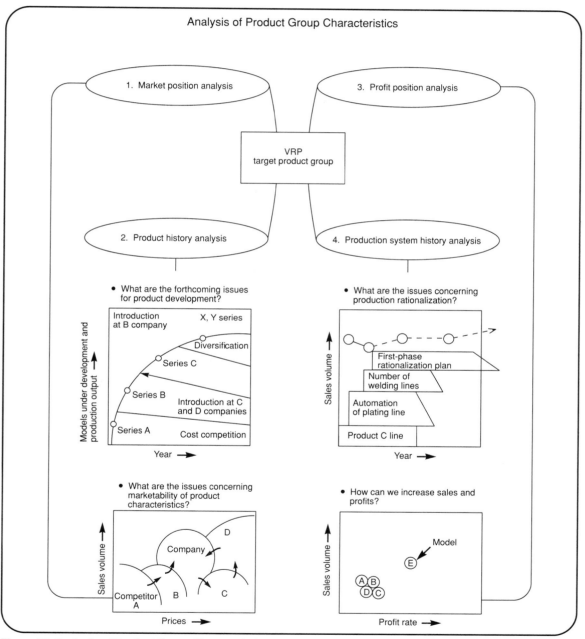

Figure 58: Analysis of Product Group Characteristics

Cost Analysis

Cost analysis has two general purposes: The first is to serve as a means of evaluating ideas proposed for reducing the number of parts and processes. The second is to help clarify the places where costs occur and the causes behind their occurrence. Figure 59 shows how cost figures can be organized into a cost analysis table.

One of the key points in cost analysis is to clarify just when and in what manner each of the compiled costs was established. Even when we narrow a cost down to a particular part, we still do not know the constituent cost factors. Moreover, people in different company divisions will naturally have different ways of dealing with the costs. Consequently, in VRP cost analysis, we must take an approach based on clear and consistent cost appraisal standards.

After organizing the cost analysis table, it is sometimes helpful to draft a Pareto diagram as an additional tool for cost analysis.

Parts Index Analysis

In parts index analysis, we look within the product group and find out how the products' parts are being used. Along with the process index analysis (described later), parts index analysis is one of the most important types of VRP analysis.

The purposes of parts index analysis are (1) to gain a quantitative grasp of the status quo, (2) to quantitatively establish targets, and (3) to clearly identify likely problem areas. Figure 60 is an example of parts index analysis, in which the vertically added amounts (in this case, seven) are the number of parts used in a particular model. In this case, then, each model consists of seven parts, and since there are five models, the total parts index is (7 x 5 =) 35. The column at the far right of the figure shows totals for the number of models in which each part is used. As shown in the figure, the "lid" part is listed as being used in four models while the lid mechanism is used in only two models. The total number of part types is shown as 13. In this case, we calculate the parts level (sum) as the product of the number of part types times the number of parts, which is (13 x 35 =) 255.

In such situations, a common VRP goal is to reduce both the number of part types and parts by 30 percent and to reduce the parts level (sum) by 50 percent.

After carrying out this analysis for all of the assembly units, we need clarify just where and how many parts occur at each assembly and strive to reduce the number of parts.

Even before entering into an analysis procedure such as the one shown in Figure 61, we must check the part nomenclature in the product structure.

We often use computers to assist in this analysis, but before doing so we must not forget to give the programmer prior notice of our need for a program to work with the data base.

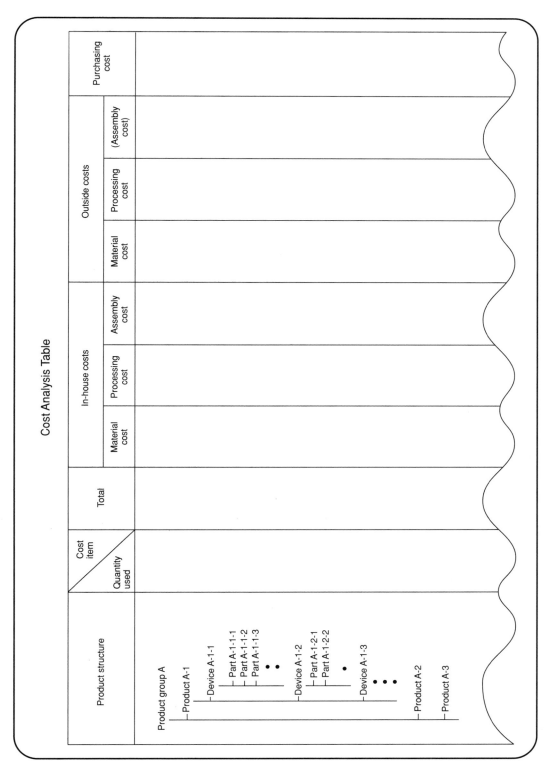

Figure 59: Cost Analysis

Parts Index Analysis

Assembly unit	Part name	Part number	Model					Total types
			A 21	A 35	B 10	C 48	D 09	
Lid assembly	Lid	1021	1	1				4
		1025			1			
		1033				1		
		1051					1	
	Lid mechanism	2118	1	1	1			2
		2147				1	1	
	Lid plate	3006	1	1	1	1	1	1
	Spring	9119	2	2				3
		9020			2	2		
		9031					2	
	Shaft	5026	2					3
		5342		2	2			
		5544				2	2	
Number of parts			7	7	7	7	7	13/35

- Total number of part types: 13
- Total number of parts: 35

Parts index: 255

Figure 60: Parts Index Analysis

Figure 62 shows an analysis worksheet that was used in an actual VRP project. This worksheet contains data on how the parts were used, how many were used, where they were ordered from, and various cost data. These data are very helpful as analytical tools when studying ways to reduce the number of parts.

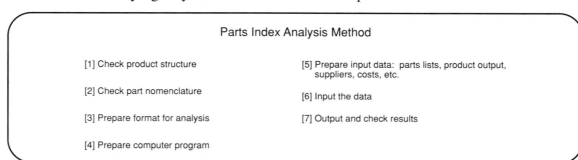

Parts Index Analysis Method

[1] Check product structure

[2] Check part nomenclature

[3] Prepare format for analysis

[4] Prepare computer program

[5] Prepare input data: parts lists, product output, suppliers, costs, etc.

[6] Input the data

[7] Output and check results

Figure 61 Caption: Parts Index Analysis Method

Parts Index Analysis Table

Assembly unit name	Constituent part			Product number					Total part types	Number used per year	Supplier code	Purchasing cost	Costs					Total costs
	Name	Number	Material	001	002	003	004	005					In-house		Outside			
													Material cost	Processing cost	Material cost	Processing cost		
									Total number of parts									

Figure 62: Parts Index Analysis Table

Production Process Index Analysis

In production process index analysis, we seek to understand how many processes and process types go into the production of the target product group. Like parts index analysis, the purpose of this analysis is to gain a quantitative grasp of both the current levels and the target level and to clarify the problem areas.

Production process index analysis is actually broken down into two analyses, one of the parts processing index and the other of the assembly processing index. The former index is based on individual parts while the latter looks at assembly units, as shown in Figure 63.

In both analyses, we add up the number of processes needed to process each part or product and to perform the necessary assembly tasks. Then we add up the types of processes and multiply them by the number of processes to obtain the production process index. We take this production process index as a quantitative expression of the current level of production processes.

In addition to the analyses just described, we can also perform process pattern analysis (such as that shown in Figure 64) and production process point analysis. These analyses provide data that can be used not only in production process analysis but also to indicate current levels when reducing the variety or number of production processes.

When performing these analyses, we must be careful to first get an accurate understanding of the current conditions. In this connection, it is vital that we take the trouble to visit the production processes concerned and have a firsthand look at them. Standards manuals are useful references, but many times the real situation is quite different from that described in the manual.

Control Point Analysis

We use control point analysis to find out exactly what control tasks are currently occurring and to calculate the quantity of control points and the amount of work and labor hours involved in each control point. In special-order type companies, where the C (Control) cost tends to take on a higher proportion of total costs than in other types of companies, this C cost plays a part in many areas targeted for cost reduction. Control point analysis can be very useful as a cost-cutting tool for such companies.

The purposes of this type of analysis are (1) to understand how it is possible to reduce the C cost along with the number and types of parts and (2) to understand how control tasks can be improved.

Figure 65 contains a description of the control point analysis method while Figure 66 lists its steps. The "influence factor" mentioned in Figure 65 means the estimated amount of reduction in control point related work time that can be expected to result

Production Process Index Analysis

(1) Parts processing process index analysis

Process	Equipment or line	A	B	C	D	E	F	G	Total types
Injection molding	a_1	3							2
	a_2		3						
Casting	b_1			3					3
	b_2				4				
	b_3					5			
Plating	c_1						2		4
	c_2								
	c_3						3		
	c_4							2	
Machining	d_1			2					6
	d_2				2	2			
	d_3			2			2	2	
	d_4				2	3			
	d_5				2				
	d_6								
Number of processes		3	3	7	10	10	7	4	$\frac{15}{44}$

Number of process types: 15	VRP process index: 660
Number of processes: 44	

(2) Assembly process index analysis

Process	Line or table	A	B	C	D	E	Total types
Assembly	a	7	7				4
	b			6			
	c				5		
	d					8	
Number of processes		7	7	6	5	8	$\frac{4}{33}$

Number of process types: 4	VRP process index: 132
Number of processes: 33	

Figure 63: Production Process Index Analysis

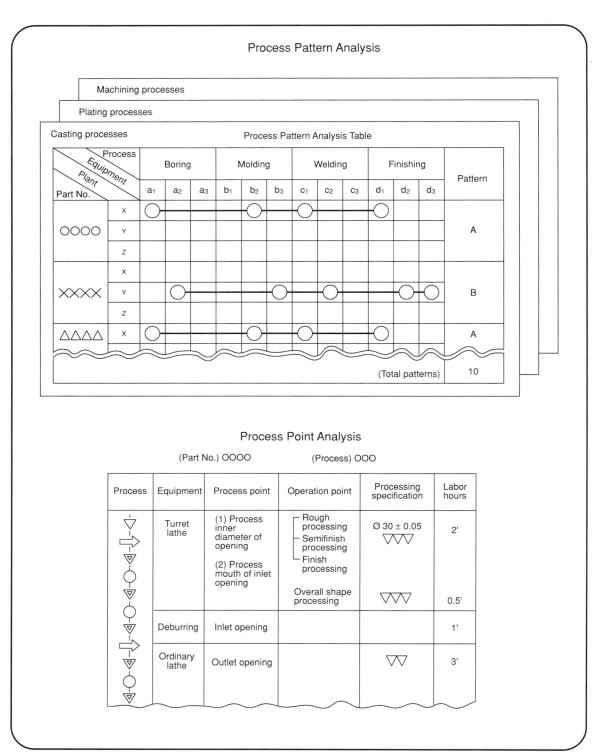

Figure 64: Process Pattern Analysis (a.k.a., Process Path Analysis)

Control Point Analysis

Division	Control point	Total work time	Influence factor	Influence time of each control type		
				①	②	③
Design	① Scheme drawings	1000H	10%	100H	0	0
	② Assembly drawings	3000H	50%	1000H	500H	0
	③ Parts drawings	⋮	⋮	⋮	⋮	⋮
	④ ⋮					
	Subtotal					
Materials	① Ordering					
	② Delivery control					
	③ Acceptance inspection					
	⋮					
	Subtotal					
Production technology						
	Total					

Figure 65: Control Point Analysis

from a given amount of reduction in the number of parts. We establish these influence factors by analyzing how work is generated and handled at each control point. Also in Figure 65, "control type" refers to the various types of control work, such as generating drawings of each part and preparing a warehousing system and a demand/supply estimation system.

[1] Basic data survey

- Work flow per control types (drawings, parts, etc.)
- Targeted C cost
- Targeted personnel total
- Current variety and number of parts

[2] Preparation for division-specific control point analysis

- Targeted people
- Measurement parameters (drawings, certain vouchers, etc.)
- Survey method (questionnaire, work sampling, etc.)
- Format

[3] Execution of control point analysis

[4] Compilation of results

Figure 66: Steps in Control Point Analysis

Breakdown of Cost Reduction Levels

Although we set target levels as a first step in our VRP project, we must break these general target levels down into more specific goals before we can undertake concrete cost-cutting activities. How we break down these target levels depends on how many product structure levels we are dealing with; as a rule of thumb, however, it is useful to begin by setting values for each block unit that includes a single function. Figure 67 shows an example of such a breakdown method. In this example, there are some areas where target values have not been set; because those areas had very low priority, they could reasonably be left unexamined.

In addition, some project teams choose to set target values that are even more difficult than the preestablished targets as a means of invigorating their team with an extra challenge.

One of the purposes for this breakdown of cost reduction goals is to help clarify which activities are to receive the greatest emphasis. Figure 68 illustrates how we establish such high-priority themes in VRP activities. As shown in the figure, we must be explicit about the items that receive a high priority, our method of emphasizing them, and our interpretation of that emphasis.

Breakdown of Cost Reduction Targets

Product group OOO　　　　Target: 20% cost reduction

Assembly	Current status	Cost reduction ratio	Cost reduction amount	Breakdown by cost category											
				Purchasing costs			Material costs			In-house manufacturing costs			Outside manufacturing costs		
				Current status	CR ratio	CR amount	Current status	CR ratio	CR amount	Current status	CR ratio	CR amount	Current status	CR ratio	CR amount
A	2000	24.8%	495	500	25 %	125	300	10 %	30	800	30 %	240	400	25 %	100
B	700	25 %	175	200	25 %	50	50	10 %	5	150	30 %	45	300	25 %	75
C	100	-	-	100	-	-	-	-	-	-	-	-	-	-	-
D	600	15.5%	93	300	20 %	60	30	-	-	120	15 %	18	150	10 %	15
E	800	17.5%	140	200	10 %	20	100	10 %	10	100	10 %	10	400	25 %	100
F	800	21.9%	175	700	25 %	175	10	-	-	-	-	-	90	-	-
	5000	21.6%	1078	2000	21.5%	430	490	9.2%	45	1170	26.8%	313	1340	21.6%	290

Figure 67: Breakdown of Cost Reduction Targets

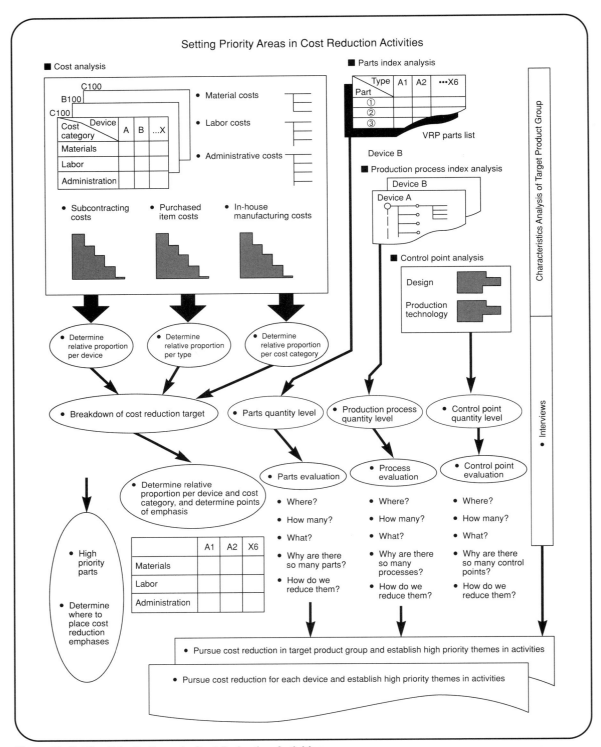

Figure 68: Setting Priority Areas in Cost Reduction Activities

CHAPTER 8

V Cost Reduction

Fixed vs. Variable Policy

Before seeking to cut the V cost that is generated by the variety of parts and production processes, we must first identify the true demands placed on the product group by the market and the company's clients, then decide as a matter of policy which parts and processes are to be fixed and which are to be variable. As described in an earlier chapter, we attempt to meet market and client needs by dealing with the three factors — *quantity, systems and specifications,* and *configuration* — that have a direct influence on the generation of variety.

In establishing such a fixed vs. variable policy, we begin by clarifying the target markets and clients from which the product needs arise. This tells us about what product model characteristics and specifications will respond to these needs.

Once we have identified these characteristics, we can list the required features in each product. In doing this, we must be careful to consider only the needs of the market and clients and not to confuse or mix these needs with those of the product designers. As shown in Figure 69, we list the identified needs along with ideas for their fulfillment, then place them along the horizontal tabulation of model groups to determine whether the required functions are fixed or variable functions.

Integration and Consolidation of Specifications and Systems Pattern

With a fixed vs. variable policy in hand, we are ready to apply the VRP techniques to increase the proportion of fixed parts while determining the basic product structure's specifications and systems.

Figure 70 shows how we first extract a pattern of specifications and systems, compare this pattern with our fixed vs. variable policy, and then study how we can integrate and consolidate the two.

The results of these study efforts will be used in establishing product specifications, so we must proceed with utmost care at this stage. We are not merely seeking to rearrange things at each level. As explained in the previous chapter, we must instead establish an integration and consolidation plan that entails new specifications and new systems in response to the actual needs of markets and clients.

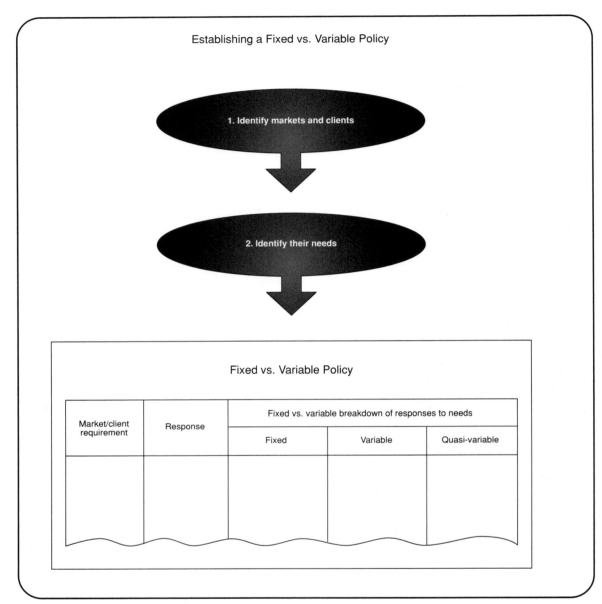

Figure 69: Establishing a Fixed vs. Variable Policy

Integration and Consolidation of Process Pattern

We also must seek to integrate and consolidate the pattern of process paths, as shown in Figure 71.

In so doing, the first important thing to note is the similarities among the various products and parts. Next, we must break our habitual way of thinking about process

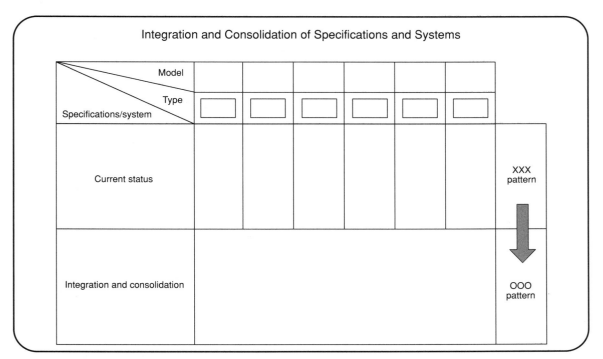

Figure 70: Integration and Consolidation of Specifications and Systems

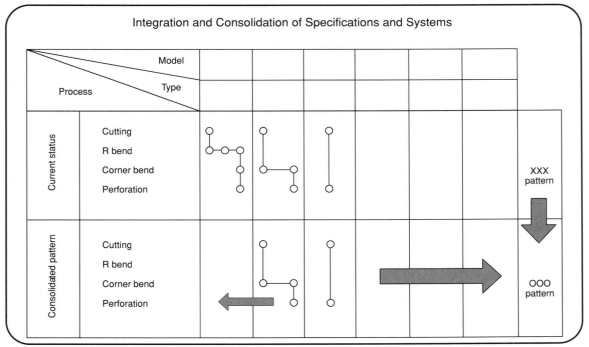

Figure 71: Integration and Consolidation of Process Patterns

patterns. If we think about them from the conventional perspective of manufacturing, we see the various restrictions that exist with regard to both "nuts and bolts" aspects such as equipment, jigs, and tools, and "abstract" aspects such as knowledge. This tends to narrow our perspective. Therefore, we must discard that way of thinking and instead take the positive view, moving toward reducing those restrictions.

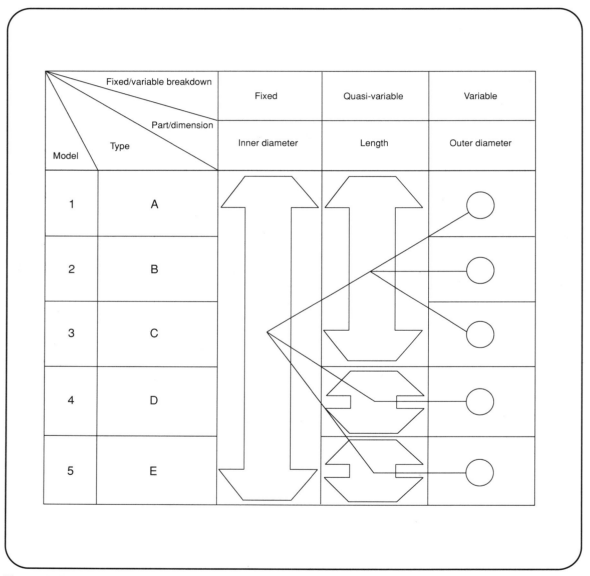

Figure 72: Applying the *Fixed vs. Variable* Technique to Parts, Dimensions, and Numerical Values

Applying the *Fixed vs. Variable* and *Combination* Techniques to Parts, Dimensions, and Numerical Values

Using our integrated and consolidated pattern of specifications and systems, we can see how to apply the *fixed vs. variable* and *combination* techniques to dimensions and other numerical values. As shown in Figure 72, the dimensions of each part have been clearly defined as belonging to a fixed, quasi-variable, or variable part.

Applying the *Fixed vs. Variable* and *Combination* Techniques to Production Processes

As with parts, we can also use our integrated and consolidated pattern of process paths in applying these two VRP techniques to determine which production processes will be fixed processes, as shown in Figure 73. Naturally, in this study we make use of the results of our *fixed vs. variable* study of product structure.

Study of V Cost Reduction Policy

We are now ready to plan a policy for reducing cost in the fixed parts we have determined based on our application of the fixed vs. variable technique to parts, dimensions, and processes. As shown in Figure 74, we take on this planning task from two angles: (1) raising production output per part and (2) increasing similarity within each process.

Compilation of Results

Figure 75 shows how we can compare the results of our efforts to current-status figures for the numbers of systems, process paths, fixed parts, fixed processes, and V cost reduction policy initiatives to obtain the respective reduction rates.

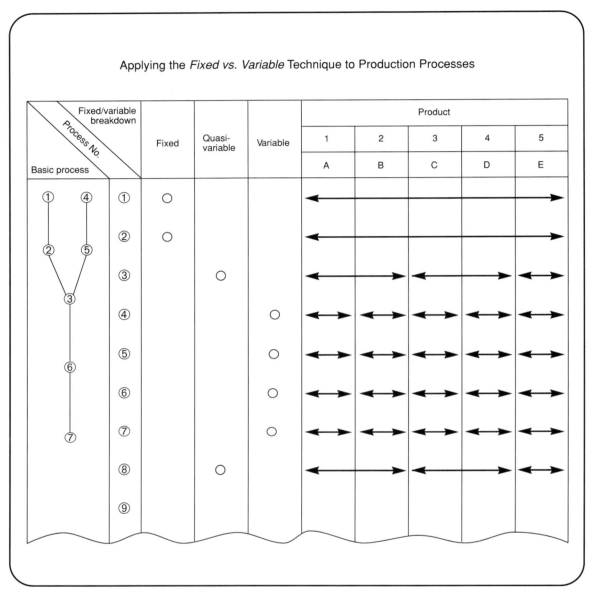

Figure 73: Applying the "Fixed vs. Variable" Technique to Production Processes

Study of V Cost Reduction Policy

(1) Policy to raise the production output per part

Fixed part items	Level of raised production output	Cost reduction policy measures
1 X X X X	☐ ⟶ ☐	① X X X X X ② X X X X X

(2) Policy to increase the amount of similarity in each process

Fixed part item	Level of increased similarity	Cost reduction policy measures
1 X X X X	☐ ⟶ ☐	① X X X X X ② X X X X X

Figure 74: Study of V Cost Reduction Policy

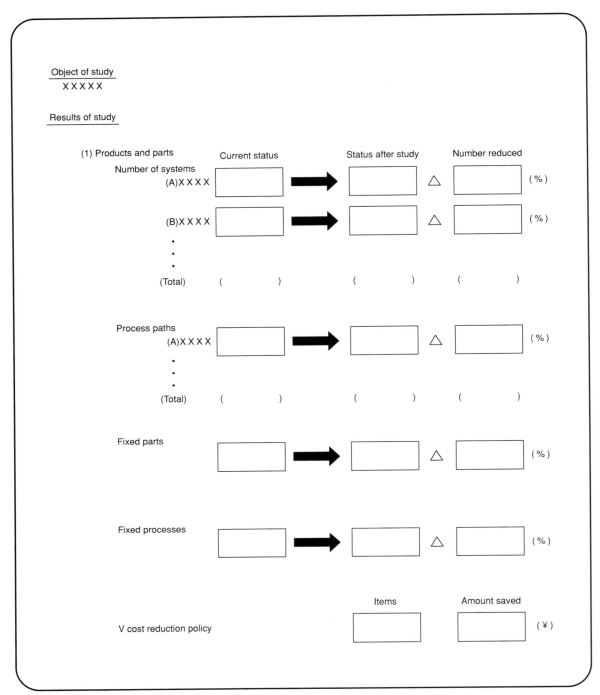

Figure 75: Compilation of Results

CHAPTER 9

F Cost Reduction

Multifunctionality and Integration

We use the *multifunctionality and integration* VRP technique to study the product structures and production processes of integrated and/or combined systems and product types as a means of reducing the F cost.

Before beginning such a study, we must consciously direct our efforts by deciding from which level to start our study (*See* Figure 76). This is what we mean by establishing a multifunctionality and integration policy.

Multifunctionality and Integration Policy			
Object of study / Study level	XXX section	XXX\ section	XXXX section
(1) Study based on specifications			
(2) Study based on functions			
(3) Study based on structures			
(4) Study based on processing and assembly methods			
(5) Study based on simplification of parts and processes			
(6) Study based on new materials and new technologies			

Figure 76: Multifunctionality and Integration Policy

Study Based on Specifications

A *study based on specifications* means a review of the specifications of current parts to find redundant or excessive specifications.

As shown in Figure 77, we must first identify the current specifications and clarify the reasons for their existence. Naturally, this means checking the appropriateness of these reasons. After making such a review, we can begin to "wash out" and eliminate superfluous specifications and study improvement proposals.

Study Based on Specifications						
Name of Assembly Unit	Name of Part	Number of Part	Current Specs	Reason for Specs	Superfluous Specs	Elimination Plan

Figure 77: Study Based on Specifications

Study Based on Functions

A *study based on functions* means overhauling the procedures — *i.e.*, the methods — by which parts and products provide the required functions. Basically, we change these methods by creating products that have fewer parts, require fewer production processes, use cheaper materials, and incur generally lower costs than do existing products. Therefore, we strive to streamline, integrate, and simplify product functions so that each part can provide multiple functions.

As shown in Figure 78, during this study we clarify the parts' functions and search for ways to increase the multifunctionality of each part.

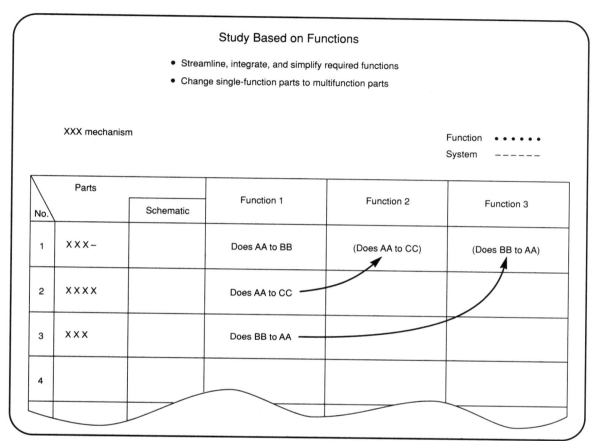

Figure 78: Study Based on Functions

Study Based on Structures

A *study based on structures* means looking at how to change the ways parts are used (are structured) to realize a certain method. To do this, we first take a structure consisting of several parts and find ways to streamline, integrate, and simplify the parts as a group of parts.

Figure 79 shows how we can lay out a grid of parts as a tool for planning their multifunctional integration.

A point of caution in this regard is that ideas which call for simplification of two current parts into one part must also produce reductions in the related material cost and the processing and assembly costs.

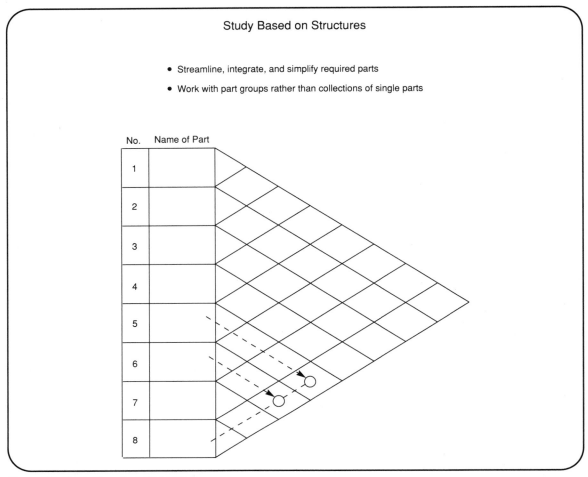

Figure 79: Study Based on Structures

Simplifying Parts and Reducing Material Costs

Here, we study ways to simplify each part and cut its material cost. In this case, simplification means making parts both "purer" and "easier." We make them "purer" by removing superfluous elements and "easier" by making them easier to use. We can compile the results of this study in the manner shown in Figure 80.

Toward Fewer Production Processes and Labor Hours

As was shown in Figure 64, VRP attempts to reduce *processes, processing points, work operation points,* and *processing specifications.* When working toward fewer production processes, we should consider:

No.	Simplification and Material Cost Reduction Ideas	Schematic	Effect
1		(Current) (Idea)	

Simplifying Parts and Reducing Material Costs

Figure 80: Simplifying Parts and Reducing Material Costs

- removing branch processes and keeping the production process flow as simple as possible,
- devising ways to use just one production method per single part,
- incorporating several operations at each process to increase process flexibility,
- getting away from functional organization of machining and assembly processes,
- reducing processes and labor hours by streamlining, integrating, simplifying, and replacing, and
- making reductions in sequence from processes to processing points to work operation points to specifications and finally to labor hours.

Figure 81 illustrates such a study for minimizing production processes and labor hours.

Summary

Figure 82 summarizes the method for establishing a multifunctional and integration policy, and lists the planned reduction amounts of parts, processes, material costs, processing costs, and labor hours.

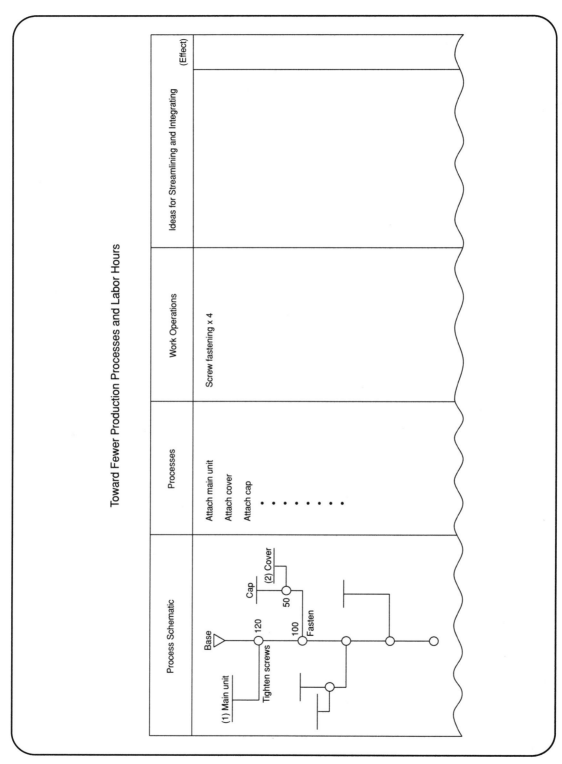

Figure 81: Toward Fewer Production Processes and Labor Hours

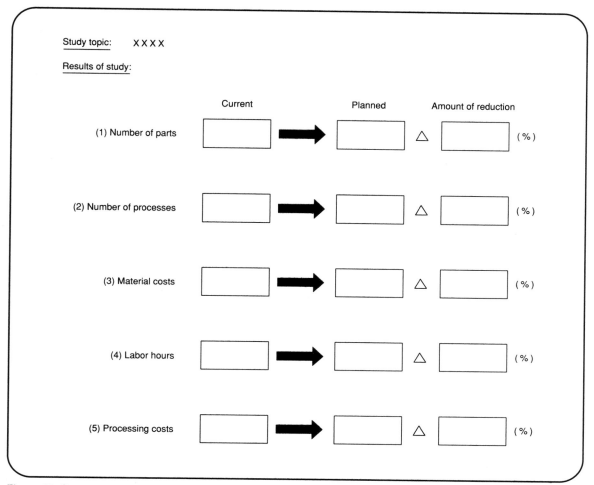

Figure 82: Summary

Selection of Parts and Processes Using the *Trend* and *Range* Techniques

The thinking behind the *trend* and *range* VRP techniques is centered on the following three points:

1. When we apply ordering principles to designs, we can reduce design-related labor hours, and eventually, we can also reduce the number of parts.
2. Applying these techniques to materials yields advantages in purchasing.
3. The techniques make both processing and assembly processes easier to perform and pave the way for upgrading equipment, jigs, and tools.

Figure 83 shows how we can apply these techniques to certain parts and clarify the process.

Selection of Parts and Processes Using the *Trend* and *Range* Techniques

Study topic: XXXX

Process \ Part	Layout	Materials	Dimensions	Shape

Figure 83: Selection of Parts and Processes Using the *Trend* and *Range* Techniques

Discovering the Effects of the *Trend* and *Range* Techniques

We must determine the current distribution of dimensional values for the items we have selected. As shown in Figure 84, when analyzing these dimensional values, we can use the principles of the *trend* and *range* techniques to establish new dimensional values. We can also clearly identify the effects of such new values.

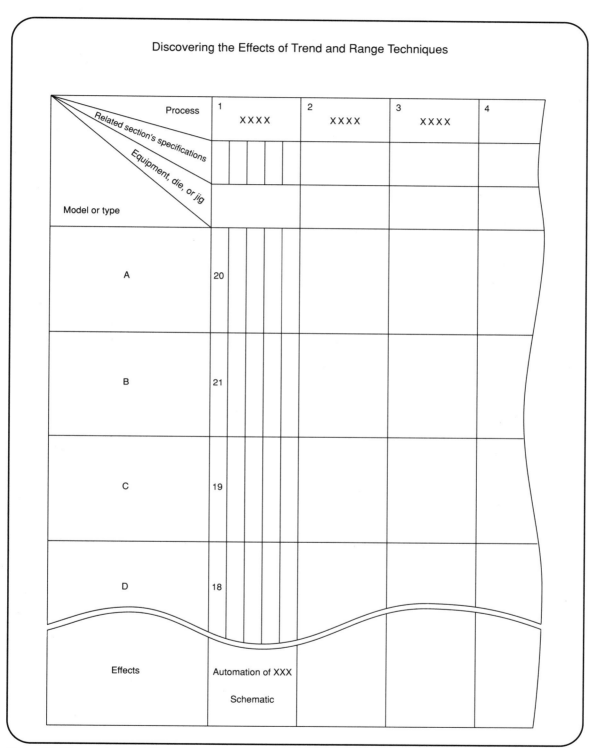

Figure 84: Discovering the Effects of the *Trend* and *Range* Techniques

CHAPTER 10

C Cost Reduction

We can produce a C cost reduction not only in terms of the decline in C cost that accompanies a shrinkage in the number of parts, but also in the C cost related to a reduction and simplification of control points.

Bringing the C Cost Down through Fewer Parts and Production Processes

A control point analysis like the one shown in Figure 85 helps clarify the work load (labor hours) required by each control point. Meanwhile, if we are successful in using the five VRP techniques to reduce the number of parts, we will also produce a decline in the amount of control point-related work load (parameters) and thereby help lower the C cost. Reductions in parts and control point-related work load do not occur at the same rate, however. We can estimate the relation between these two types of reductions in terms of their influence factors (which control point analysis also helps us to understand).

As a result, we can understand how to reduce the C cost corresponding to each control point, as shown in Figure 85.

Division	Control Point	Parameters	Total Time (Labor Hours)	Influence Factor	Parameters after VRP	Total Time (Labor Hours) after VRP	Amount of C Cost Reduction

Figure 85: C Cost Reduction through Fewer Parts and Production Processes

Bringing the C Cost Down through Control Point Integration and Simplification

After the work load-related C cost has been reduced as an effect of lowering the numbers of parts and production processes, we can still carry out improvements in the control flow and in each control point to further shrink the C cost.

As shown in Figure 86, we can do this by eliminating imbalances in control point-related work loads and control flow patterns and by finding ways to integrate control points. Next, we can try to upgrade our control point work processing system by investigating further reductions.

Division	Control Point	Parameters after VRP	Total Time (Labor Hours) after VRP	Current Processing System	Ideas for Integrating Control Points	Ideas for Simplifying Control Points

Figure 86: C Cost Reduction through Control Point Integration and Simplification

CHAPTER 11

Summary and Evaluation of Product and Production Process Ideas

At this stage, we bring together the various concepts and ideas concerning products and production processes that have been proposed during our multifaceted studies, calculate their total effect, and evaluate them.

Summary of Product and Production Process Ideas

We first compile all of the improvement ideas that were generated as we applied the five VRP techniques in our studies.

To begin with, we bring the fixed vs. variable ideas and the parts reduction ideas together in the manner shown in Figure 87.

Next, we gather the production process-related system ideas, layout drawings, work operation ideas, and equipment/jig/tool ideas as shown in Figures 88 and 89.

At the evaluation step, we evaluate the overall cost reduction amount, the parts index, and the process index, as shown in Figure 90.

We use the items generated at the project planning stage as the evaluation items.

In addition, we should clarify any qualitative effects that may occur.

Compilation of Product-Related Ideas

- Fixed vs. variable specifications: all fixed vs. variable ideas, ranging from systems to part dimensions

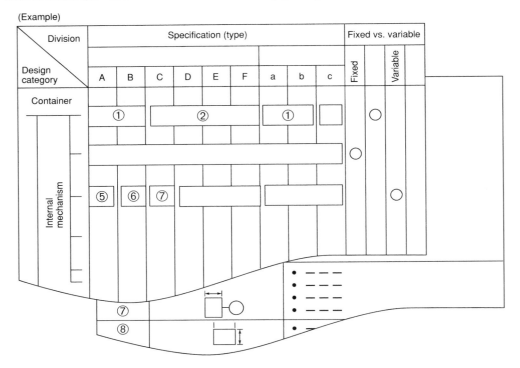

- Plan for halving the number of parts: clarify the image of VR-type products, then implement the plan.

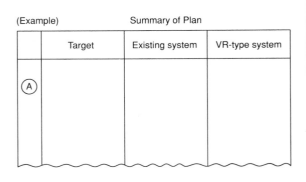

Figure 87: Compilation of Product-Related Ideas

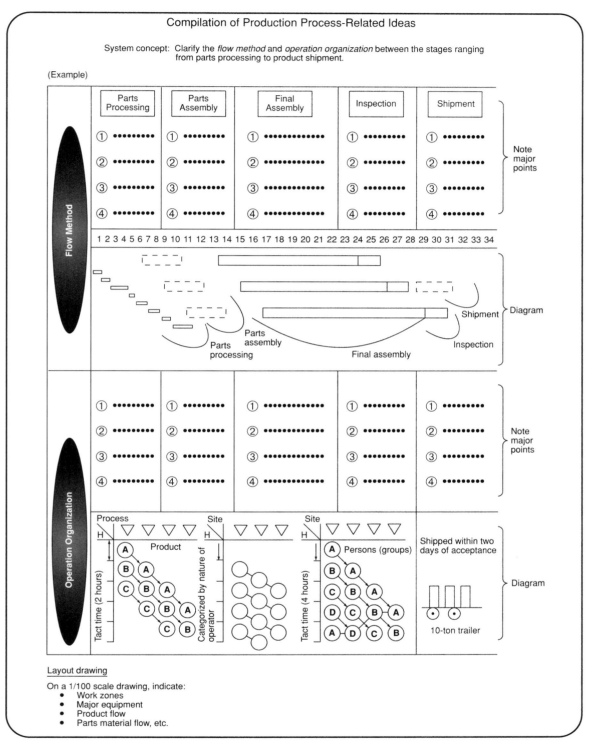

Figure 88: Compilation of Production Process-Related Ideas

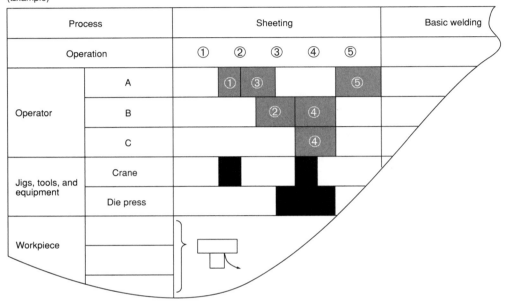

Compilation of Production Process-Related Ideas

Operations manual: explains the processes, work operations, required time, required personnel, jigs, tools, and work responsibilities.

(Example)

Process		Sheeting					Basic welding
Operation		①	②	③	④	⑤	
Operator	A	①	③			⑤	
	B			②	④		
	C				④		
Jigs, tools, and equipment	Crane						
	Die press						
Workpiece							

Equipment and jig manual: explains new and improved equipment, the target workpieces, the costs, effects, handling methods, acquisition procedure, etc.

(Example)

Division	Topic	Policy	Equipment Name	Investment Amount		Estimated Effect (¥10,000/year)	Recovery period (years)	Schedule: Order reception to completion
				Number				
		••••••	•••••	1	(unit: ¥10,000) 800	Material cost		/12 E
		••••••	••••	1	2,000	2,507		~
		••••••	•••••	2	1,800	Processing cost 1,113		/6 E
			Subtotal		4,600	3,620	1.27	

In connection with the above study, we should list all equipment, jigs, and tools by what is required and what is not required.

Figure 89: Compilation of Production Process-Related Ideas

Evaluation

Study Topic: X X X X X

Effect item / Effect	Current	New	Amounts of costs and effects
1 Direct material cost			
2 Direct labor cost			
3 Variable expenses			
4 No. of equipment units in next year			[1],[2],[3] Effect amount x [4]
5 Design and testing costs			
6 Die and jig costs			
7 Parts index (No. of parts x types of parts)			
8 Process index			

Cost 1: items 1, 2, 3
Cost 2: item 4
Cost 3: items 5, 6
Indices: items 7, 8

Note: Effect and cost estimate values are for all types together.

Total effect amount = (cost 2)
Required cost = (cost 3)

Figure 90: Evaluation

CHAPTER 12

Detailed Design and Preparation for Implementation

At this stage, we draw up a detailed implementation plan, set up an organization for such implementation of the selected ideas and plans, and begin concrete preparation activities as well as detailed design and prototype testing.

Detailed Design of Products and Production Processes

As shown in Figure 91, we try to diagram and make specifications for all of the ideas we have adopted concerning products and production processes. In the case of products, we use drawings such as prototype drawings. Consequently, we have to look closely at the dimensional relationships in the drawings, clarifying any technical hurdles that must be cleared. Some of these hurdles can be approached as prototype test items, and others as subproject themes.

In the case of production processes, we can examine the selected ideas in detail as layout drawings or organizational drawings that include the lines, equipment, staff, and parts supply system. As for specifications, we need to finalize the skill specifications, operation format specifications, and major equipment specifications before we can reach the target production output. In addition to elucidating any technical problems, we must set up pilot lines and subproject themes to deal with such problems.

Inaugurating the Implementation Plan and Subproject Themes

As we prepare for implementation, we must clarify just what we are about to do, when we need to do it by, and what kind of organization we will have for doing it.

Figure 92 provides an example of an implementation plan that includes separate daily schedules for product-related and production process-related development activities. The timing of production process-related development requires careful attention, since these activities include some items that are realized only after new products are brought on line and some that are directly related to production itself.

At the same time, we can be working out schedules for advancing the subproject themes we had elucidated at the *detailed design* stage. Figure 93 (page 124) describes examples of typical subproject themes.

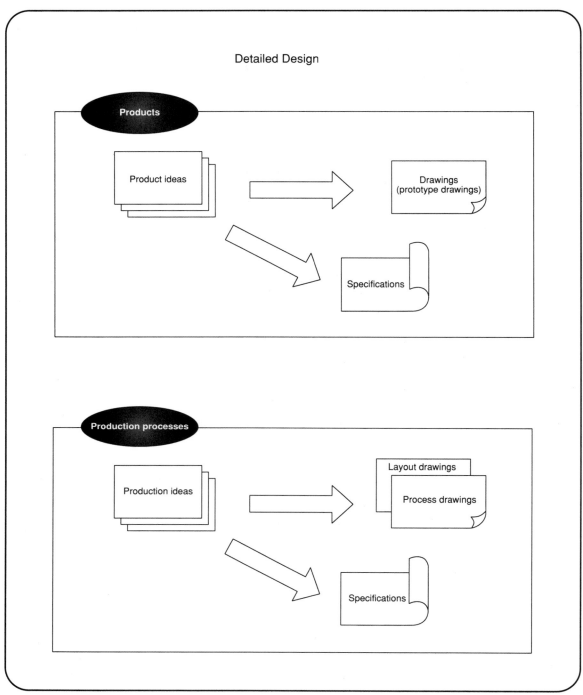

Figure 91: Detailed Design

In working out the subproject theme advancement schedules, we go into even greater detail than at the project conceptualization stage but also maintain a wide perspective in our deliberations. We must, for instance, account for the interrelations among production lines. To do this, we should provide opportunities for staff education and orientation sessions and should emphasize the need for fresh ideas and wide use of new technologies.

Implementation Plan

(1) New Model Development Plan

Model Name	Description of Development	Goal	Schedule
○○○○	(1) XXX device XXX function		Test design → Testing → Large-scale testing

(2) Production Process Development Plan

Target Process	Description of Development	Goal	Schedule

Figure 92: Implementation Plan

Implementation Follow-up

Implementation activities are centered on divisions that have not had success in previous implementation efforts. Consequently, such implementation is carried out by the members of the division concerned. The follow-up, however, is also done as part the VRP project, and in this follow-up we try to efficiently and promptly apply the basic concepts of VRP. Ordinarily, VRP follow-up teams begin their work somewhere between three and six months after completion of implementation. Figure 94 shows an example of VRP follow-up activities.

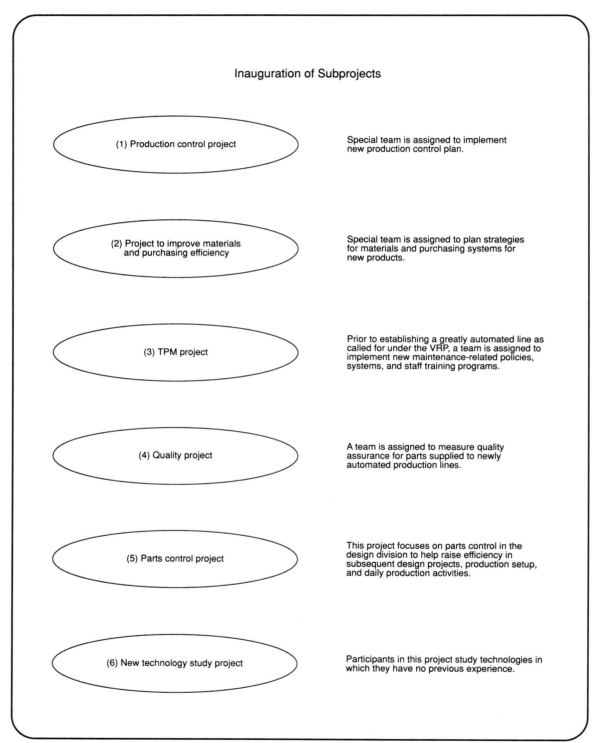

Figure 93: Inauguration of Subprojects

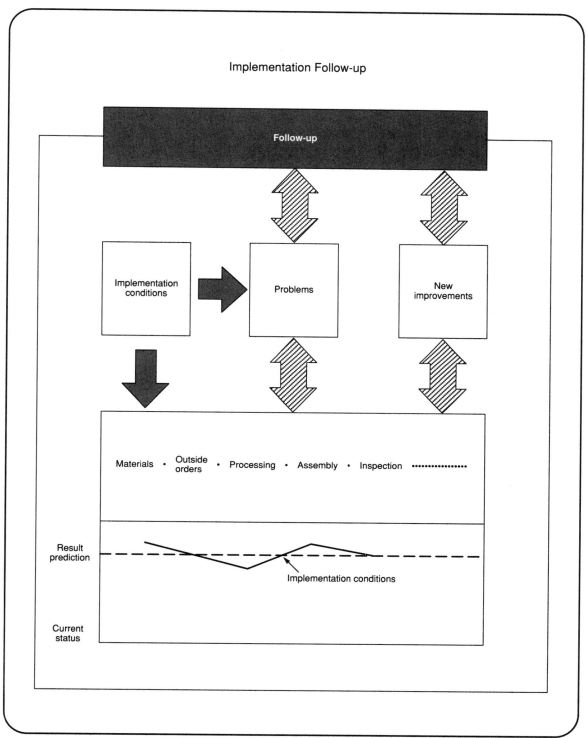

Figure 94: Implementation Follow-up

PART IV

Examples of VRP Application

We all tend to think of our own company as different from others. While competitors *try* to keep pace with us, we consider *our* company to have a unique structure, one that sets it apart. Such an attitude, however, either prevents needed steps from being taken or quickly nips them in the bud.

It is true that no two companies are alike because products, output, and personnel all differ. That is no excuse, however, for not making an effort to improve the efficiency of one's business. The key to a successful enterprise is its persistence in clarifying and solving its own problems.

In this section we shall examine some specific examples of VRP's implementation: C corporation, a major electrical appliance manufacturer; G corporation, a manufacturer of automobile components; and L and M corporations, electrical parts manufacturers. Let's see how each company came to grips with its particular problems.

CHAPTER 13

Four Case Studies

Case Study #1: A 30 Percent Market Share with a New Model

C Corporation is a major manufacturer of electrical appliances. With an annual output of 200,000 units, it once boasted a 30 percent share of the kitchen appliance market. A flood of competing products, however, pushed it down to 20 percent, and in 1983, the kitchen appliance division was on the brink of going into the red. Top management decided to completely renovate both the product and its production line.

An all-out VRP project

This VRP project began with a core team of four members, all managers of their departments: project leader M, engineering manager, manager B from production engineering, manager G from the design department, and manager J from marketing. Members were added as needed from these departments.

Manager M had been in charge of the design of the latest line of kitchen appliances. It was painful for him to see his own products declining in the marketplace in the wake of aggressive price-cutting by rival manufacturers. Voluntarily, he chose to head the VRP project and vowed to spend as many hours in the project room as time permitted.

The project began in early fall. It was physically located in a space created at the center of the design department; the designers' desks encircled the project room, thus making it the focus of their work environment. The purpose of this layout was to facilitate an all-out design engineering offensive. C Corporation was placing all its bets on the VRP project. It had already anticipated and obtained the investment required to bring the project to fruition. The level of expectation engendered by this one project can be inferred from a comment heard frequently from those outside the project: "How will we manage until the new product comes out?"

C Corporation chose VRP as the means to carry out this project because general manager M had a friend at a company that had previously implemented VRP. M had not only listened to his friend but had visited the plant to see the results for himself. Realizing that the problem his friend's company had solved was identical to the one faced by C Corporation, he decided that VRP's goals perfectly matched those of the new project he was hoping to start.

The mutual problem was the ongoing proliferation of product variety responding to a diversifying market. At C Corporation, despite M's efforts, the market share of existing products was being whittled away by the competition. Every time his division created a new product, it broke even — but production systems became more complex and profitability of old products decreased.

Overall, the appliance division was barely breaking even. Older products, meanwhile, were neglected by both production and marketing, eventually losing their market share to rivals' lower-priced goods. The company found itself in a vicious cycle: when market share fell, product variety was increased; preexisting products were neglected, causing their market share to lose more ground than the new products gained; product variety was then increased, repeating the cycle. In short, the company could not efficiently meet the need for diversification.

What and how many to make, and how to make them

Phase 1 of a VRP project is setting targets. In the case of C Corporation, the first target was a market share of 30 percent, a figure based on what C Corporation could legitimately expect given its marketing power and brand name image. The output necessary to meet this share of the market was set at 300,000 units per year. Meanwhile, manufacturing cost targets required an 8 percent reduction in material costs and a 17.8 percent reduction in assembly costs. Also, the product line would be expanded from the current two, to four products.

These Phase 1 target figures exceeded those originally projected by C Corporation. The company had decided on an approach exactly opposite to that of expanding its product series from two to four. Originally, it was hoping to consolidate its two series into one. The results of VRP analysis, however, showed that a 30 percent market share could not possibly be secured with one series.

The analysis performed during Phase 1 also elicited the following project guidelines:

1. Introduce the concept of *fixed vs. variable* in products.
2. Apply the same concept to the factory.
3. Install an integrated case production line, automate it as fully as possible, and make it the core of the production line.
4. Simplify the surface treatment process.
5. Develop a product plan that permits automation of at least half of each subassembly process line in tandem with the case line.
6. Reduce the number of assembly lines.
7. Simplify the materials and parts supply system.
8. Undertake a detailed study of policy vis-à-vis subcontractors beginning with Phase 2.

The total number of parts was 11,736, and that of processes was 1,807. After analyzing the particulars of each quantity, we concluded that both should be reduced by half.

Redesigning a product for automation

After entering the Phase 2 plan development stage, the first task was to design a product structure to facilitate the reduction of the total number of parts. At the same time we evaluated the resulting lineup of finished products. We then identified fixed and variable portions in each product.

Product group configuration required the greatest adjustment. What cost price should be assigned to which class of products? Which specific components should serve as the basis for cost variance? We had to define differences between products. Marketing chief J found the collection of data for analysis to be extremely difficult because the company had never formulated a plan like this before. He had to make numerous visits to the sales department before a policy on product criteria was finally established. It became apparent that no one knew whether the long history of product changes had improved or worsened existing product groups. This state of affairs was a major problem for C Corporation.

In keeping with the guidelines of Phase 1, we devised a product structure that was best adapted to automation. This automated product structure was naturally applied fundamentally to fixed portions. We studied manual processes to provide flexibility for variable portions. Figure 95 illustrates the resulting product plan.

Case Study #2: Building a New Plant with VRP

G Corporation is a midsize manufacturer of automobile components. The VRP project implemented by this company took three years to complete and encompassed new plant construction, including the clearing of land for the site.

Radical reform

The environment of the automobile industry is perennially a harsh one, buffeted from year to year by demands for lower costs, higher quality, and new technology. Anticipating increasingly tough industry conditions, G Corporation decided to implement a plan for strengthening its organizational structure. The concept was to use its cramped older plant for new products while building a new plant for the leading product line. They planned to incorporate VRP simultaneously to restructure their production system. VRP was chosen because of precedents showing its successful application to the auto industry.

Their goal was an increase of at least 8 percent in gross profits. That goal led company executives to examine all possible means. The project team, led by a senior executive, included two designers, two production engineers, one production manager, and a group in charge of plant construction. The goal assumed new plant construction.

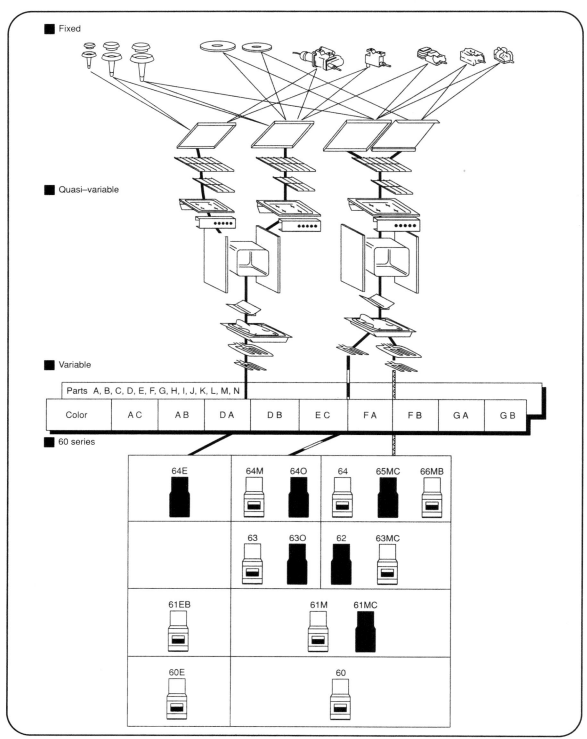

Figure 95: Fixed vs. Variable Product Plan

The ultimate in new plant construction

An automobile component constitutes only one part or unit of a finished car. Its structure is naturally affected by the design concept for that entire car. Such a unit must be designed within defined limits and must be completely redesigned with every major model change. The finished product usually changes every four years so that the chance to make changes comes only once in four years. Any attempt to renovate the entire automobile would require a good ten years of planning.

Therefore, a VRP project for developing a product structure oriented to the needs of the entire car must take into account both long-range plans and minor day-to-day improvements.

In terms of product design, the dominating factor in finished car specifications is the same as that of any other product: it must fit specific market needs. Product design, however, differs in that those needs cannot be defined in a vacuum. Depending on our perspective, having someone else decide those limits for us, even providing actual specifications, makes our job that much easier.

In the case of the unit manufactured by G Corporation, we were able to identify a fixed portion applicable to all car models; a quasi-fixed portion common to models of a given grade; and a variable portion that accommodated the peculiarities of each individual model. These distinctions formed the basis of our new product plan.

The pivotal point in this VRP project was the restructuring of production processes made possible by the construction of the new plant. First we developed plans to automate 30 percent of all processes. Excluding assembly processes, this automated 22 out of a total of 72 processes. Added to 13 existing processes, this brought the number of automated processes to 35, or 49 percent of the total.

The improvements we made resulted in an 8.6 percent reduction in material costs. Total number of parts fell by 28 percent.

We were also able to reduce the number of processes by simplifying 14 process points, drastically cutting inventories through the synchronization of operations, and minimizing transport work. These improvements in the production system then facilitated the reduction of the labor force by 120 workers, or 48 percent of its original size. This figure takes into account the in-plant absorption of previously subcontracted work as well. The overall result was right on target: an 8 percent improvement in gross profits.

Because these plans could be implemented only as changes were made to the product over time, it took three years to see their full effect. During that period, output increased by 45 percent, so the final results actually exceeded target figures considerably.

Meanwhile, the move to the new plant required detailed planning. One year after the inauguration of the VRP project, members of the design department returned to their old jobs, the project room was rechristened the "new plant preparation room," and new members were added. The preparation room members moved into the new plant the following year.

Case Study #3: VRP for Individually Ordered Products

M Corporation is a maker of heavy electrical equipment. Most of its products are big, made–to–order machines with individual specifications. The company, however, does have a basic product, or product concept, with annual orders in the 100 to 200 range at most. Applying VRP to this type of product requires a slightly different approach than might be applied to mass-produced, high–volume goods. With every order received, M Corporation must run the entire gauntlet from design through production.

Preventing specification variety from affecting design and production

The subject of this VRP project was control units for large equipment installed in office buildings. Because the control units were built to individual orders and specifications, nearly all aspects of their manufacture — from design through materials procurement and processes other than processing and assembly — required considerable labor power. Processing and assembly, as well, consisted mostly of manual operations. Repeated piecemeal efforts at improving efficiency had reached an impasse, while the variety of customer specifications continued to increase.

The key question is "Where are the standardized points, and how can we exploit them?" The project's goal was to develop design and production methods for making products that met individual requirements, without carrying their attendant variations over into the design and production processes themselves. We accomplished this by analyzing the relationship between specifications and structure in previous designs, identifying fixed portions that could be added or deleted in the design process, and correlating these to the actual product structure.

We developed a production format that allowed this process to begin as soon as an order was received. As a result, we were able to reduce the time required for design and production from 185 to 100 days. We reduced required labor by almost half — 49 percent. By the project's end, the number of processes dropped from 1,114 to 620.

This particular project was characterized by a product subject to individual orders and specifications. Our experiences so far have shown that the most unique product or process inevitably contains some portion that is not unique.

When this VRP project reached the implementation stage, the same company inaugurated a CAD (computer–aided design)-editorial design project.

Case Study #4: Implementing an Integrated Line

L Corporation makes a wide variety of electrical components such as switches, plug sockets, and safety lamps. Though diversified, it is a high-volume, mass–production outfit with an annual output of several million units. Unlike previous examples, L Corporation's VRP project deliberately increased the number of processes to achieve newly integrated preassembly processes.

Choices for a model plant

For the manufacturer of a tremendous variety of products, the reasons for starting a VRP project were complex. Naturally, L Corporation wanted to raise profit margins. The primary motivation, however, was to employ untried methods to manufacture a new product series under development. They wanted to use the new factory as a model for the corporation's other undertakings.

The initial job of deciding which model product group should be incorporated in the new model plant took some time. The one selected had its basic design complete but still allowed room for structural variations. It could be produced in quantities of close to 10 million units, suitable for the new model plant. This particular product group comprised 45 product types with a total of 230 parts.

In the Phase 1 planning stage, we set these policy guidelines:

- From the standpoints of technology and efficacy, integrate parts processing into the assembly plant to the greatest degree possible.
- Try to automate assembly processes.
- Organize a special team for quality improvement.

We set targets of reducing the workforce by half, the inventory by a quarter, and defects by half. The project was scheduled to take a year and a half.

An assembly line of 25 automatic assembly machines

Because of our decision to integrate parts processing, the total number of processes for this plant actually increased. After working on the simplification of extant assembly processes, however, we formulated a plan to use automatic assembly machines for the entire line beyond the injection machine and up through the cardboard boxing stage. Those sections that proved technically troublesome were returned to the drawing board to be redesigned for automation. This operation cost about ¥ 250 million ($1.08 million). Except for materials cost, this amount consisted entirely of expenses for in-house design, processing, assembly, and equipment procurement.

Parts quality is the biggest problem associated with this kind of line, because the efficiency of an assembly machine depends on the quality of the parts that enter the feeder. Therefore, we set up a quality improvement team within the VRP project to deal exclusively with this problem. Nevertheless, reaching our targeted operating rate of 85 percent still took six months from startup. Reducing this period probably would have required a complete reassessment of all parts processing processes.

By focusing on fixed portions, we also reexamined product concepts with an eye to automation. A few products and parts whose functions or market requirements necessitated a large number of variable portions still required manual processing, however.

This project achieved its target figures with some variation, and the company recovered its investment in a year and a half.

PART V

Conditions for Success

It should be clear from the foregoing description that VRP is not merely a method for reducing costs, but a basic approach for systematizing products and production. At the same time, it allows for product diversification while radically reorganizing a company's products and production systems. Consequently, VRP's success depends on several conditions.

CHAPTER 14

Requirements for a Successful VRP Program

For a successful VRP program, the following requirements are necessary:

(1) Top managers responsible for products and production must be committed to the program.

VRP returns to the basics to renovate products and production systems. The effect yields a clear difference in a company's break-even point. It also fundamentally changes product design, thus making VRP's influence felt in the marketplace. This can lead to a number of problems.

For example, to supply service parts for already delivered products, company catalogs could require rewriting. A revised catalog might point out variations in features available based on a clear identification of fixed and variable components, or offer a choice of different combinations.

Changes in product design also affect production organization. They may alter the ratio of in–house and subcontracted work or require investments in plant and equipment. Product evaluation will require trial production and testing. The cooperation of clients may be needed. Therefore, it is essential that top managers — managing directors, operations division chiefs, plant managers, design and production engineering department heads — make the final decision to introduce VRP.

(2) The company must select a product group range and workplace suitable for VRP application.

A company should not abruptly apply VRP to every one of its plants and products and then expect beneficial effects across the board. Most companies have a sizable number of products still in the early stages of development that do not show any problematic variety. Some will eventually even be discontinued.

In addition, product groups may have entirely different uses, be based on different design principles, or be made in different plants. These disparities make the selection of appropriate product groups and plants a crucial factor in VRP's success.

Too narrow a selection can limit the scope of VRP concept application and, hence, limit its effect as well. At the same time, too broad a selection will cause a lack of focus and results that are at best superficial.

The products and plants to which VRP is to be applied must therefore be selected with great care. One rule of thumb is to deal only in units for which VRP effects can be assessed on a break-even chart.

(3) Target levels must be clearly defined.

Any project must define its goals before it can move forward. VRP is no exception. While, in theory, VRP's aim is fundamental reform, in practice, the improvement level of products and production systems depends on the results desired by the company — such as a specific percentage cost reduction. A quantitative description of the target is therefore of great relevance in setting and implementing policy, as well as in defining how far to carry out reforms and in evaluating and adhering to that policy when ready for implementation. *(See* Figure 96.)

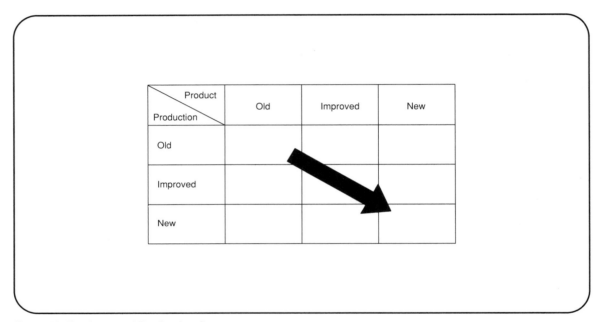

Figure 96: Products and Production Systems

The level of reform will be determined both by what is necessary and what is feasible. This underscores the importance of VRP's Phase 1 analysis of the status quo.

(4) The company must establish an interdepartmental organization of the VRP project that includes designers and production engineers.

VRP does not succeed when based on input from specialists in only one field. People who understand products, markets, production, materials, and subcontracting are all needed. Because production control, cost control, and quality control will also be affected, a VRP project must have members with a variety of backgrounds and viewpoints. Whether a given member works full-time or part–time on the project depends on the priorities and structures of the project.

As the project proceeds, membership will change in size and personnel. Design personnel usually take top priority in the beginning, with more emphasis placed on production people in the project's later stages.

Good management is essential to the organization of a VRP project, and selecting a good project leader is a key ingredient.

(5) The company must have firmly established procedures for implementing the VRP project.

A VRP project can last anywhere from six months to two years. When they first launch the project, both top management and project members are apt to look for quick results. They may be tempted to bypass the analysis that is needed and apply VRP's five concepts to the products already on hand. This shortcut must be discouraged.

The reasons are obvious: While extant designs and production systems may contain some valuable, well–thought out elements, wishful thinking can also cloud perception of the current variety. As a result, enthusiasm for basic reform may be somewhat lacking. A VRP project must therefore start with a careful analysis of things as they are and then devise its concepts on the basis of that analysis before going on to detail design. The project must subsequently undergo a thorough evaluation before it can be implemented successfully.

(6) Reform must be based on the hands-on application of VRP's five concepts

The five concepts are not the only approaches or methods applied by VRP to reorganize products or production systems. Value engineering (VE), standardization, industrial engineering (IE), and automation are other approaches that should be used.

The five concepts *are* extremely effective in resolving the key conflicts between standardization and diversification, and between simplification and complexity. By analyzing conditions and formulating plans, VRP project members should become so thoroughly acquainted with these five concepts that they begin to view everything around them in such terms. Getting to that point requires commitment and training.

(7) Participation and decision–making by management must occur at each stage of a VRP project's implementation.

VRP is a method of reorganization — and, as such, its failure may spell deep trouble. Judging just how far to pursue this reorganization requires an evaluation of the alternatives, the efficacy, the scale of investment, and the predicted results of such a project. Quite often, companies will compare two or three alternative proposals before making a decision.

Consequently, at every stage of a VRP project, it is crucial that team members await a thorough evaluation and decision by management before proceeding to the next phase.

(8) The company must develop detailed plans to cover all aspects of VRP implementation.

The reforms instigated by VRP are far-reaching: Blueprints must be redrawn; prototypes must be tested; tools and dies must be remodeled; equipment must be ordered. When an actual switchover takes place, items that are — and are not — interchangeable must be handled differently than before. Workers' duties may also change radically. So will the production control database, the flow of products, and inventory handling. All of this requires education in the workplace. Consequently, implementation of VRP should begin only after thorough planning has been completed.

(9) The company must make a dispassionate evaluation of the results of VRP's implementation vis-à-vis its original targets.

We can verify the effects of a VRP project by comparing the data collected after its implementation with (1) the data collected and analyzed at its inception, (2) the data created in the plan-drafting and detail design stages, and (3) the data used in the evaluation process. VRP may well produce results beyond those originally intended. The following comments have all been heard at companies after they implemented VRP:

- "Our approach to design underwent a fundamental change when we began dealing with diversification in terms of fixed and variable portions and combinations."
- "Drawing control became less of a chore because we realized that only a relatively small number of drawings was necessary."
- "In the production engineering department, we were able to apply VRP to tools and dies. We recently have begun making our own VRP dies in response to the diversification of requirements, thereby keeping die costs down."
- "A third of our factory space opened up, and we have recently put it to use in the manufacture of another new product."
- "Stocks have been reduced drastically. The savings alone, calculated in terms of interest, will allow us to recover our VRP expenditures within three years."
- "The workplace is less cluttered, making it easy to see what's going on just by walking around. This kind of hands-on management makes the elimination of needless variety essential."
- "We've noticed that the drastic reduction in the number of parts has improved product reliability. Complaints and requests for service parts have fallen far below previous amounts."
- "We've been able to keep service parts inventories down. Before VRP, the rapid proliferation of service parts with every new product had us worried."

CHAPTER 15

Advances in VRP

VRP provides us with a strategy for getting at the root of the problem of product diversification, as well as a set of basic concepts for implementing that strategy. As such, VRP contains the potential for developing in a number of directions.

VRP and Logistics

According to a contemporary view of product costs, we must consider the total life cycle costs incurred from a product's inception to its demise, as shown in Figure 97. This viewpoint and the techniques associated with it are known as *logistics*.

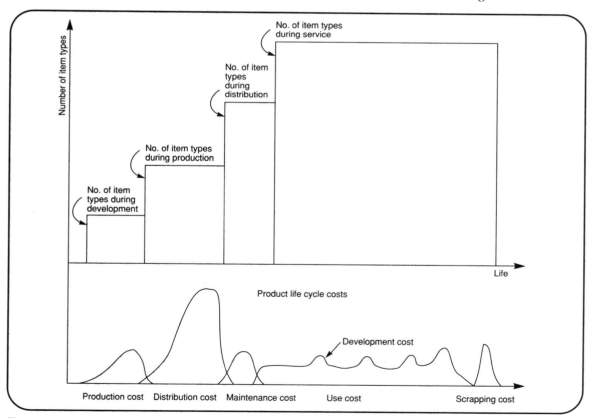

Figure 97: Life Cycle Costs and Number of Managed Items

Sweden, the first country outside Japan to evaluate VRP, treated it as one form of logistics. Viewed over time, the variety of items to be managed is greater for production than for development, and still greater for maintenance, which must supply service parts for as long as seven years after a product has been discontinued.

This suggests the enormity of the management problems associated with the number of components involved — both the number of part types specific to each product group and the part types common to all product groups. From the standpoint of logistics, then, VRP is a very effective technique.

VRP and Product Reliability

We had the opportunity to hold a lecture and discussion on VRP for the managers in the product development division of an electrical appliance manufacturer. At this meeting, the executive in charge stated that "VRP is a method of increasing product reliability." We recognized that this appraisal of VRP as a means of quality improvement — not simply cost reduction — was extremely significant.

He explained that in applying multifunctionality in order to actively reduce the number of parts, VRP also reduces the opportunities for breakdowns or defects in products that have grown too complex as a result of being upgraded. The application of fixed vs. variable analysis to optimize the use of fixed portions in different product types enhances reliability because it increases the use of proven parts and units. Combination, then, is extremely effective in improving both reliability and maintenance because it facilitates the use of interchangeable units.

Editorial Planning and Development

As mentioned in the third case study, VRP evolved from *editorial design* as a response to situations in which product diversification was already rampant. Now, however, we must ask how VRP can be used to deal with future product development.

As consultants, we have answered this question recently by developing a new set of concepts and methods as further steps in the advancement of editorial design and VRP. These new concepts are called *editorial planning* and *editorial development*. We begin by planning the product groups to be developed over the next several years. The products are subjected to grouping and editing at this initial planning stage. In other words, group development is assured through the integration of VRP concepts and editorial design in the planning process.

This method has already effectively reduced labor and development time required for development design, trial production, and testing. When one company substituted editorial planning and development of its product line for its previous one–piece–at–

a–time development practices, it reduced development labor hours by 30 percent and development time by 50 percent.

Factory Automation and VRP

We mentioned earlier that VRP helps to prevent factory automation (FA), CAD/CAM, and other such systems from becoming empty slogans and to guarantee the return on investment in them. Businesses that successfully implement FA first make an effort to reduce their equipment and tooling. Although the concepts of *fixed–vs.–variable* and *combination* were originally aimed at reducing parts to cope with product variety, their application to production systems will certainly optimize FA efficiency as well.

FA has been a topic of consideration primarily in the machine industry. Recently, however, the need for flexible production in the processing industry has created a growing demand for variety. The resulting application of VRP concepts has given birth to FA methods for manufacturing industries.

In one such case, a confectioner applied VRP concepts to determine which production processes should be used for handling a variety of candy fillings. We now advise processing industries on how to use VRP to institute factory automation.

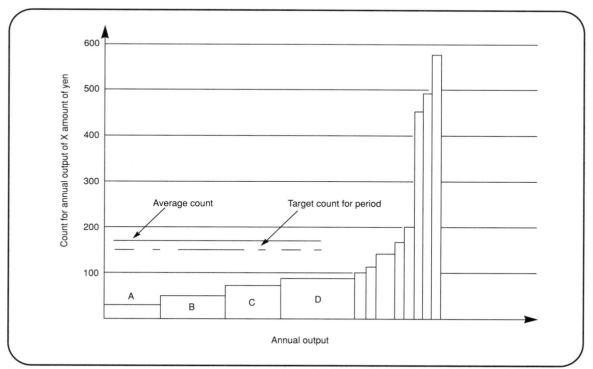

Figure 98: "Parts" and Product Output

Typen und Teile, Group Technology, and VRP

Typen und teile (TUT), which means "types and parts," is a method of reducing parts and products developed by the Siemens Company of West Germany. It divides products into "types," counts each movement generated in managing the component parts of a given type — procurement, storage, storage removal, and so forth — as one "part," and adds up the total parts per type. It then compares sales with parts by calculating the number of parts per sales unit, and tabulates the results, as in Figure 98. These data aid in the decision–making analysis for scrapping products or reducing the number of parts.

A meeting with Siemens to exchange information on VRP and TUT gave rise to a valuable discussion about the benefits of TUT as a management method and VRP as a reduction method, and the possibility of combining these two approaches.

Although not directly related, Group Technology (GT) also aims to deal systematically with diversified parts and units by classifying and organizing them, then seeking ways to reduce them or to replicate similar components. GT, TUT, and VRP all serve as means of systematization in response to variety, and all share the same ends. Of the three, VRP takes the most positive approach by providing concrete concepts and methods for reducing variety.

Finally, VRP application also facilitates CAD/CAM development.

Conclusion

A large number of products have already achieved wide dissemination. New products penetrate the market with ever-increasing rapidity. The concentrated export of a commodity to a single country is no longer feasible, however competitive the product. Consumers are quick to express their personal likes and dislikes through their purchase decisions. In our information-intensive society, both the speed with which information is both transmitted and becomes obsolete continues to increase.

Any way you look at it, the demand for greater variety is still rising.

But is the variety we now have of real value to the consumer? Is it not in fact a chaotic jumble originating in pressures felt by manufacturers and distributors? Doesn't this variety respond in a fragmented manner to too many individual demands? Can service parts effectively be supplied for the market life of such products?

Finally, hasn't the need for greater production flexibility resulted in a pursuit of automation based on academic notions that ignore the realities of business and on a limited view of its application to the production equipment industry?

One of the tasks before us is to achieve genuine factory automation while incorporating an orderly process of diversification. Such a process should provide flexibility based on eliminating useless variety and bringing to light the variety that really counts. Toward this end, and to conserve precious resources, the popularization and advancement of VRP are of critical importance.

About the Authors

Toshio Suzue

Mr. Suzue joined the Japan Management Association in 1973 where he did management consulting on production engineering management and labor-saving practices. He developed variety reduction in 1975. He currently consults for JMA Consultants Europe and is chief consultant with Japan Management Association Consulting, Inc.

He is the author of the MCB report *Variety Reduction* and various essays.

Akira Kohdate

Mr. Kohdate joined the Japan Management Association in 1953. As a management consultant, he conducted studies and provided guidance in the areas of design management and R&D management at over 100 companies. He developed concepts of design management in 1959. He visited U.S. and European research institutes in 1964, developing R&D management concepts. In 1968 he studied group technology (GT) and developed editorial design. He did consulting work with Toshio Suzue in France in 1981 and founded JMA Consultants Europe in 1984. Mr. Kohdate is executive director of Japan Management Association Consulting, Inc. and a principal consultant at the RD&E Center.

His publications and translations include *Design Management*, *Efficient Research and Development*, and numerous essays.

Index

Other Books on Just-In-Time

Productivity Press publishes and distributes materials on continuous improvement in productivity, quality, customer service, and the creative involvement of all employees. Many of our products are direct source materials from Japan that have been translated into English for the first time and are available exclusively from Productivity. Supplemental products and services include newsletters, conferences, seminars, in-house training and consulting, audio-visual training programs, and industrial study missions. Send for our free book catalog.

JIT Factory Revolution
A Pictorial Guide to Factory Design of the Future
Hiroyuki Hirano / JIT Management Library

Here at last is the first-ever encyclopedia picture book of JIT. Using 240 pages of photos, cartoons, and diagrams, this unprecedented behind-the-scenes look at actual production and assembly plants shows you exactly how JIT looks and functions. It shows you how to set up each area of a JIT plant and provides hundreds of useful ideas you can implement. If you've made the crucial decision to run production using JIT and want to show you employees what it's all about, this book is a must. The photographs, from various Japanese production and assembly plants, provide vivid depictions of what work is like in a JIT environment. And the text, simple and easy to read, makes all the essentials crystal clear.
ISBN 0-915299–44–5 / 218 pages / illustrated / $49.95 / Order code JITFAC-BK

Kanban and Just-In-Time at Toyota
Management Begins at the Workplace (rev.)
edited by the Japan Management Association, translated by David J. Lu

Based on seminars developed by Taiichi Ohno and others at Toyota for their major suppliers, this book is the best practical introduction to Just-In-Time available. Now in a newly expanded edition, it explains every aspect of a "pull" system in clear and simple terms–the underlying rationale, how to set up the system and get everyone involved, and how to refine it once it's in place. A groundbreaking and essential tool for companies beginning JIT implementation.
ISBN 0-915299-48-8 / 224 pages / $34.95 / Order code KAN-BK

Non-Stock Production
The Shingo System for Continuous Improvement
by Shigeo Shingo

Shingo, whose work at Toyota provided the foundation for JIT, teaches how to implement non-stock production in your JIT manufacturing operations. The culmination of his extensive writings on efficient production management and continuous

improvement, his latest book is an essential companion volume to his other books on other key elements of JIT, including SMED and Poka-Yoke.
ISBN 0-915299-30-5 / 480 pages / $75.00 / Order code NON-BK

Poka-Yoke
Improving Product Quality by Preventing Defects
compiled by Nikkan Kogyo Shimbun, Ltd./Factory Magazine (ed.), preface by Shigeo Shingo

If your goal is 100% zero defects, here is the book for you—a completely illustrated guide to poka-yoke (mistake-proofing) for supervisors and shop-floor workers. Many poka-yoke devices come from line workers and are implemented with the help of engineering staff. The result is better product quality—and greater participation by workers in efforts to improve your processes, your products, and your company as a whole.
ISBN 0-915299-31-3 / 288 pages / $59.95 / Order code IPOKA-BK

Management for Quality Improvement
The 7 New QC Tools
edited by Shigeru Mizuno

Building on the traditional seven QC tools, these new tools were developed specifically for managers. They help in planning, troubleshooting, and communicating with maximum effectiveness at every stage of a quality improvement program. Just recently made available in the U.S., they are certain to advance quality improvement efforts for anyone involved in project management, quality assurance, MIS, or TQC.
ISBN 0-915299-29-1 / 318 pages / $59.95 / Order code 7QC-BK

TPM Development Program
Implementing Total Productive Maintenance
edited by Seiichi Nakajima

This book outlines a three-year program for systematic TPM development and implementation. It describes in detail the five principal developmental activities of TPM:

1. Systematic elimination of the six big equipment related losses through small group activities
2. Autonomous maintenance (by operators)
3. Scheduled maintenance for the maintenance department
4. Training in operation and maintenance skills
5. Comprehensive equipment management from the design stage

ISBN 0-915299-37-2 / 528 pages / $85.00 / Order code DTPM-BK

TO ORDER: Write, phone, or fax Productivity Press, Dept. BK, P.O. Box 3007, Cambridge, MA 02140, phone 1-800-274-9911, fax 617-868-3524. Send check or charge to your credit card (American Express, Visa, MasterCard accepted).

U.S. ORDERS: Add $4 shipping for first book, $2 each additional. CT residents add 8% and MA residents 5% sales tax.

FOREIGN ORDERS: Payment must be made in U.S. dollars (checks must be drawn on U.S. banks). For Canadian orders, add $10 shipping for first book, $2 each additional. For orders to other countries write, phone, or fax for quote and indicate shipping method desired.

NOTE: Prices subject to change without notice.

Productivity Press, Inc.
Dept. BK, P.O. Box 3007
Cambridge, MA 02140
1-800-274-9911

Complete List of Titles from Productivity Press

Asaka, Tetsuichi and Kazuo Ozeki (eds.). Handbook of Quality Tools: The Japanese Approach
ISBN 0-915299-45-3 / 1990 / 325 pages / $59.95 / order code HQT

Buehler, Vernon M. and Y.K. Shetty (eds.). Competing Through Productivity and Quality
ISBN 0-915299-43-7 / 1989 / 576 pages / $39.95 / order code COMP

Christopher, William F. Productivity Measurement Handbook
ISBN 0-915299-05-4 / 1985 / 680 pages / $137.95 / order code PMH

Ford, Henry. Today and Tomorrow
ISBN 0-915299-36-4 / 1988 / 286 pages / $24.95 / order code FORD

Fukuda, Ryuji. CEDAC: A Tool for Continuous Systematic Improvement
ISBN 0-915299-26-7 / 1990 / 156 pages / $75.00 / order code CEDAC

Fukuda, Ryuji. Managerial Engineering: Techniques for Improving Quality and Productivity in the Workplace
ISBN 0-915299-09-7 / 1984 / 206 pages / $34.95 / order code ME

Hatakeyama, Yoshio. Manager Revolution! A Guide to Survival in Today's Changing Workplace
ISBN 0-915299-10-0 / 1985 / 208 pages / $24.95 / order code MREV

Hirano, Hiroyuki. JIT Factory Revolution: A Pictorial Guide to Factory Design of the Future
ISBN 0-915299-44-5 / 1989 / 218 pages / $49.95 / order code JITFAC

Japan Human Relations Association (ed.). The Idea Book: Improvement Through TEI (Total Employee Involvement)
ISBN 0-915299-22-4 / 1988 / 232 pages / $49.95 / order code IDEA

Japan Management Association (ed.). Kanban and Just-In-Time at Toyota: Management Begins at the Workplace (Revised Ed.), Translated by David J. Lu
ISBN 0-915299-48-8 / 1989 / 224 pages / $36.50 / order code KAN

Japan Management Association and Constance E. Dyer. The Canon Production System: Creative Involvement of the Total Workforce
ISBN 0-915299-06-2 / 1987 / 251 pages / $36.95 / order code CAN

Jones, Karen (ed.). The Best of TEI: Current Perspectives on Total Employee Involvement
ISBN 0-915299-63-1 / 1989 / 400 pages / $175.00 / order code TEI

Karatsu, Hajime. Tough Words for American Industrry
ISBN 0-915299-25-9 / 1988 / 178 pages / $24.95 / order code TOUGH

Karatsu, Hajime. TQC Wisdom of Japan: Managing for Total Quality Control, Tranlated by David J. Lu
ISBN 0-915299-18-6 / 1988 / 136 pages / $34.95 / order code WISD

Lu, David J. Inside Corporate Japan: The Art of Fumble-Free Management
ISBN 0-915299-16-X / 1987 / 278 pages / $24.95 / order code ICJ

Mizuno, Shigeru (ed.), Management for Quality Improvement: The 7 New QC Tools
ISBN 0-915299-29-1 / 1988 / 318 pages / $59.95 / order code 7QC

Monden, Yashuhiro and Michiharu Sakurai (eds.). Japanese Management Accounting: A World Class Approach to Profit Management
ISBN 0-915299-50-X / 1989 / 512 pages / $49.95 / order code JMACT

Nakajima, Seiichi. Introduction to TPM: Total Productive Maintenance
ISBN 0-915299-23-2 / 1988 / 149 pages / $39.95 / order code ITPM

Nakajima, Seiichi. TPM Development Program: Implementing Total Productive Maintenance
ISBN 0-915299-37-2 / 1989 / 528 pages / $85.00 / order code DTPM

Nikkan Kogyo Shimbun, Ltd./Factory Magazine (ed.). Poka-yoke: Improving Product Quality by Preventing Defects
ISBN 0-915299-31-3 / 1989 / 288 pages / $59.95 / order code IPOKA

Ohno, Taiichi. Toyota Production System: Beyond Large-Scale Production
ISBN 0-915299-14-3 / 1988 / 163 pages / $39.95 / order code OTPS

Ohno, Taiichi. Workplace Management
ISBN 0-915299-19-4 / 1988 / 165 pages / $34.95 / order code WPM

Ohno, Taiichi and Setsuo Mito. Just-In-Time for Today and Tomorrow
ISBN 0-915299-20-8 / 1988 / 208 pages / $34.95 / order code OMJIT

Psarouthakis, John. Better Makes Us Best
ISBN 0-915299-56-9 / 1989 / 112 pages / $16.95 / order code BMUB

Robson, Ross (ed.). The Quality and Productivity Equation: American Corporate Strategies for the 1990s
ISBN 0-915299-71-2 / 1990 / 512 pages / $29.95 / order code QPE

Shingo, Shigeo. Non-Stock Production: The Shingo System for Continuous Improvement
ISBN 0-915299-30-5 / 1988 / 480 pages / $75.00 / order code NON

Shingo, Shigeo. A Revolution In Manufacturing: The SMED System, Translated by Andrew P. Dillon
ISBN 0-915299-003-8 / 1985 / 383 pages / $70.00 / order code SMED

Shingo, Shigeo. The Sayings of Shigeo Shingo: Key Strategies for Plant Improvement, Translated by Andrew P. Dillon
ISBN 0-915299-15-1 / 1987 / 208 pages / $39.95 / order code SAY

Shingo, Shigeo. A Study of the Toyota Production System from an Industrial Engineering Viewpoint (Revised Ed.),
ISBN 0-915299-17-8 / 1989 / 352 pages / $39.95 / order code STREV

Shingo, Shigeo. Zero Quality Control: Source Inspection and the Poka-yoke System, Translated by Andrew P. Dillon
ISBN 0-915299-07-0 / 1986 / 328 pages / $70.00 / order code ZQC

Shinohara, Isao (ed.). New Production System: JIT Crossing Industry Boundaries
ISBN 0-915299-21-6 / 1988 / 224 pages / $34.95 / order code NPS

Sugiyama, Tomo. The Improvement Book: Creating the Problem-free Workplace
ISBN 0-915299-47-X / 1989 / 320 pages / $49.95 / order code IB

Suzue, Toshio and Akira Kohdate. Variety Reduction Program (VRP): A Production Strategy for Product Diversification
ISBN 0-915299-32-1 / 1990 / 325 pages / $59.95 / order code VRP

Tateisi, Kazuma. The Eternal Venture Spirit: An Exeuctive's Practical Philosophy
ISBN 0-915299-55-0 / 1989 / 208 pages / $19.95 / order code EVS

Audio-Visual Programs

Japan Management Association. Total Productive Maintenance: Maximizing Productivity and Quality
ISBN 0-915299-46-1 / 167 slides / 1989 / $749.00 / order code STPM
ISBN 0-915299-49-6 / 2 videos / 1989 / $749.00 / order code VTPM

Shingo, Shigeo. The SMED System, Translated by Andrew P. Dillon
ISBN 0-915299-11-9 / 181 slides / 1986 / $749.00 / order code S5
ISBN 0-915299-27-5 / 2 videos / 1987 / $749.00 / order code V5

Shingo, Shigeo. The Poka-yoke System, Translated by Andrew P. Dillon
ISBN 0-915299-13-5 / 235 slides / 1987 / $749.00 / order code S6
ISBN 0-915299-28-3 / 2 videos / 1987 / $749.00 / order code V6

To Order: Write, phone, or fax Productivity Press, Dept. BK, P.O. Box 3007, Cambridge, MA 02140, phone 1-800-274-9911, fax 617-868-3524. Send check or charge to your credit card (American Express, Visa, MasterCard accepted).

U.S. Orders: Add $4 shipping for first book, $2 each additional. CT residents add 7.5% and MA residents 5% sales tax.

Foreign Orders: Payment must be made in U.S. dollars (checks must be drawn on U.S. banks). For Canadian orders, add $10 shipping for first book, $2 each additional. For orders to other countries write, phone, or fax for quote and indicate shipping method desired.
Note: Prices subject to change without notice.